When I needed a criminal defense attorney for a family member, I was advised to consult various legal professionals. Bob Hartmann was the top recommendation from numerous respected attorneys, making our choice easy and one I am still grateful for today. Bob's trustworthiness, extensive knowledge, and strong ethical standards are remarkable. From the moment we contacted him, he was responsive, provided essential insights, and clearly explained our next steps. Throughout the two-year case, Bob maintained excellent communication and delivered exceptional service and results. Although no one wishes to go through the court system, having Bob Hartmann as your advocate is invaluable. He is truly the gold standard in his profession.

— K.H.

During one of the most terrifying moments our family has ever faced, when my husband was arrested at work and suddenly facing charges that carried the possibility of more than ten years in prison, Bob Hartmann provided clarity, calm, and steady guidance when we needed it most. Bob took the time to help us truly understand the charges and the legal process, explaining that the case was not simply about guilt or innocence, but about what could realistically be proven. With his experience and strategic insight, he guided my husband toward a decision that ultimately resulted in a reduced sentence of six months of house arrest, allowing him to continue working, remain at home with our children, and continue providing for our family. Without Bob's counsel, we would not have known how to navigate such a complex and emotionally overwhelming situation or make decisions based on what was truly best for our family. In our darkest and most frightening moments, Bob was available, responsive, and unwaveringly professional, providing a level of support and advocacy we will always be grateful for. Thank you, Bob!

—T.B.

MAKING IT
RAIN

THE ART OF BUILDING
A SUCCESSFUL LAW PRACTICE

MAKING IT RAIN

ROBERT HARTMANN, ESQ.

HARTMANN
LAW FIRM

Making It Rain
The Art of Building a Successful Law Practice

Published by Hartmann Law Firm.
Costa Mesa, CA, U.S.A.

HARTMANN
LAW FIRM

LAW / General Practice
LAW / Legal Profession
BUSINESS & ECONOMICS / Development / Business Development

Editing: Karen Hunsanger
Proofreading: Terry Stafford
Book Design: PearCreative.ca

Quantity Purchases: Companies, professional groups, schools, clubs, and other organizations may qualify for special terms when ordering quantities of this title. For information, email admin@hartmannlawfirm.net.

Hartmann, Robert, Author
Making It Rain
Robert Hartmann
Library of Congress Control Number: 2025924333
ISBN: 979-8-9935700-0-6 (paperback)
ISBN: 979-8-9935700-1-3 (hardcover)
ISBN: 979-8-9935700-2-0 (ebook)

This book is printed in the United States of America.

To my daughter, Sarah, my "why" and who followed in my footsteps, and to those attorneys who long for genuine work-life balance yet remain tethered to the relentless demands of law firm life because the words "I don't know how to bring in my own clients" feel heavier than any hope of independence, this book is for you.

AN INVITATION

Being a good lawyer is no longer enough. Research, writing, and analysis can be automated or outsourced. What can't be replaced is your ability to attract the right clients, earn trust quickly, and build relationships that sustain a profitable practice over time. That's rainmaking—and it starts the moment you decide to build your own firm.

I've created **The Law Firm Startup Checklist** to help you make the right decisions before costly mistakes take hold. It reflects what I've learned over nearly four decades in practice and more than 200 jury trials—what actually drives growth, leverage, and long-term stability, not theory or law school assumptions.

If you want control over your career, your income, and your time, this checklist will help you start with the right framework. Download it below and keep reading to begin building a practice clients trust, referral sources return to, and you can sustain for the long haul.

CONTENTS

FOREWORD

Every attorney eventually faces the same challenge: They know how to practice law, but no one ever taught them how to build a practice. Most respond by focusing harder on billable hours or waiting for referrals that never come. This book offers a better, more human path—one rooted in empathy, intentionality, and real-world rainmaking.

As a marketing coach who has spent years helping attorneys grow thriving practices, I've watched countless lawyers struggle with business development. Most of them don't have a plan or strategy for growing their practice. They typically "wing it" and fully rely on their intelligence—instead of a plan. I met Bob in a networking group and recognized he was the real deal. He walked the walk and talked the talk.

What sets this book apart is how real and field-tested it is. Bob doesn't teach theory—he teaches what he has lived as a criminal defense attorney who built a successful practice from scratch. Read this book, and you'll learn how to build meaningful relationships, generate referrals naturally, and show up as the lawyer people trust first. These are skills every attorney needs—and few ever learn.

I personally watched Bob apply these strategies and become more intentional in his relationships. He wasn't just meeting people, he was connecting with them. He wasn't just hoping for referrals; he was earning them. One moment stands out: I remember watching Bob seamlessly turn a simple conversation into the beginning of a long-term referral partnership—not through selling, but through genuine curiosity and generosity. That is Bob's gift, and it's the heartbeat of this book.

If you're an attorney—especially one who feels stuck, overwhelmed, or unsure of how to grow, start with the chapters on empathy, networking, and rainmaker mindset. Keep a notepad handy. Map out the relationships you want to deepen. Track the small habits that build trust. Every principle in this book can be put into practice immediately.

I'm glad this book exists. It's clear, actionable, and rooted in decades of real experience. Bob has seen what works, what doesn't, and what truly matters.

Turn the page and let him guide you toward becoming the kind of lawyer clients remember, trust, and recommend.

Gary Johnson
Founder of J2 Marketing Consultants
Phoenix, AZ
January 2026

INTRODUCTION

Most lawyers lose a trial long before the closing argument—some even before the opening statements. Sometimes the loss happens in a moment so fast that the attorney doesn't even know it went down.

I witnessed that situation materialize recently while waiting for my daughter to be sworn in as a lawyer.

We were sitting in a courtroom watching a trial in progress. The judge presiding was someone I've known for over thirty years; a respected federal judge with a national reputation. The courtroom was packed. It was beautiful, formal, and carried the weight you feel when you're in federal court. Suits and ties—a quiet tension in the air. You could tell this case was serious business.

And then it happened.

As we sat there, the trial moved forward. The judge ruled on an objection. "Sustained." One of the attorneys pushed back, and the judge repeated, "Sustained." Still, the attorney kept pushing. She accused the judge of being unfair and violating her client's rights. And she did it all in front of the jury. At one point, the judge asked her to display an exhibit on the screen, and she refused.

I leaned over to my daughter and said, "Watch the jury." Their body language immediately shifted. A few looked away. Some leaned back in their chairs, creating space between themselves and the attorney. That's a *tell.* When jurors pull back like that, they're uncomfortable.

Now imagine asking the same jury to award your client money after you've alienated them. It doesn't work. That kind of behavior doesn't just hurt your case; it hurts the profession. And what struck me most was how unnecessary it all was. The attorney could've said, "Your Honor, I respectfully disagree, but I'll comply." That's how you do it. You don't argue with a judge in front of a jury, and you certainly don't refuse to follow the judge's polite request.

I don't know if it's about experience, age, or just common sense. But I turned to my daughter and whispered, "This is your first day as a lawyer. Watch what's happening. This is how you lose a trial even before closing arguments."

Eventually, the judge called a break so he could perform my daughter's swearing-in. The judge has a great sense of humor and was kind enough to make a point. The first thing he said was, "I'm so sorry you had to see that."

I joked, "No, actually, it was perfect for her to see something like that today." He smiled and said, "You know, you're right," and we both laughed.

But I meant it. That scene captured exactly what I hope to impart to you.

Merriam-Webster defines a *rainmaker* as "a person who brings in new business; also, a person whose influence can initiate progress or ensure success."

To be a successful rainmaker, you must master skills that the lawyer in the courtroom that day clearly did not have.

We watched that lawyer insult a very well-respected judge. Believe me, you don't have to agree with every ruling on every objection, but you must act like a professional. In my view, the lawyer did not. It was the afternoon session, so presumably everyone was refreshed. Still, she completely lost control. There was just no excuse for it. And I wouldn't be surprised if she lost the jury, not because of the strength or weakness of the evidence, but because the jury couldn't get past her behavior.

We only saw a small fraction of the trial, but *the damage the attorney caused her client was obvious*. The jury had disengaged. Unfortunately, I've also seen it happen in my own closings. If a juror starts checking their watch or looking around the room, I know I've lost them. When that happens, I have a trick. I walk up to the jury box and place my hand firmly on the rail. Just enough to bring them back. You have to be present. You have to read the room.

This attorney didn't. She just kept going, unaware she was losing them.

That's what this book is really about—learning to make it rain and build a successful law practice, by protecting your clients and your reputation. And here's the truth: Most of the skills you need weren't covered in law school.

- Awareness
- Understanding
- Empathy
- Integrity
- Reliability
- Knowing how to carry yourself in a way that helps your client instead of hurting them

Your tone, your attitude, the way you treat people—those things matter. It's not just about being right. It's about being effective.

Later that day, I told my daughter, "I may not be good at everything, but reading a room, keeping my composure, and reading judges and juries—I know how to do that. And it's one of the most important skills you'll ever need as a lawyer."

There's always a better way to handle conflict. The best part of that moment was seeing in real-time a jury turn away from a lawyer who had no idea she was losing them. And once it happens, it's hard (sometimes impossible) to get them back.

We're in a profession where how you act often determines whether people listen to you or shut down. Some behaviors build credibility. Others destroy it. It's not just about what you say, it's how you say it.

Lawyers are already working from a deficit in the court of public opinion. Doctors are at the top. Attorneys are near the bottom. Why? Because we're seen as dishonest, greedy, and difficult. We're known for not calling clients back. For fighting over nonsense. For over-billing. For making problems worse, not better.

In too many cases, that reputation is earned.

Now that I have a daughter in this field, I want her to practice law in a better world. I also want the same for you. But that world doesn't yet exist, not consistently. The bad behavior of a few high-profile lawyers drags the rest of us down. The State Bar reacts by piling on rules and regulations that frustrate even good lawyers. The media pick up on the worst examples, and the public becomes even more cynical. It becomes cyclical.

If I can avoid hiring a lawyer, I will, is the sentiment today.

The law, however, is still a noble profession. It should command respect. When lawyers speak, we should be taken seriously, not brushed off or joked about. People shouldn't hear "lawyer" and roll their eyes. The perception can change, but only if more of us choose to act with integrity.

It starts with empathy. Not just for your clients, but for judges, juries, and other lawyers, too. If more attorneys brought that mindset into their practice, it would transform our profession.

So, if you want to build a *successful* solo firm, if you want to become a rainmaker, and if you want to practice law with more freedom and less friction, you're in the right place.

You don't have to stay in a job where you feel underpaid, undervalued, and overworked. You don't have to work for a boss who drains you, or at a firm that doesn't reflect your values. You don't have to stay in a type of law that no longer excites you. You just need a few key things: the confidence to go out on your own, the skill to build relationships, and the mindset to treat people well along the way. If you can master those, you will succeed.

If you're an attorney feeling stuck or burned out, you're not alone. I've been there. You don't have to stay there.

RAINMAKING EQUALS VALUE

If you can bring in business for the firm you're working for, then you're valuable. Even if you aren't needed to write a brief, you are bringing in money. And maybe down the line, you'll do it well enough to become a partner. Or maybe you stick around a few years, and the firm benefits from the business you bring in before you move on. But if you *can't* make it rain, what's the point of the firm hiring you?

If you are currently an associate at a firm, AI might be putting your job in danger. (I'll discuss AI more in Chapter 9.) But if you're a rainmaker—or if you're planning to go out on your own, then your value increases.

In today's legal climate, the ability to generate business is going to be essential if you want to get hired and have any chance to succeed at a law firm. The partners no longer need you for the research and writing. What they need is someone who can bring in clients.

And if you're starting your own firm, then you must be a rainmaker. That is a non-negotiable.

YOU DIDN'T LEARN IT IN LAW SCHOOL

Running a business and bringing in clients is more of an art than a science. For attorneys who want to leave firms or public defender offices, there really isn't anything out there that teaches the skill set they need to be more than mediocre at running their own business. It takes a certain type of personality and a specific skill set to truly be successful.

That's why there aren't many highly successful criminal defense attorneys in private practice. There are far more civil attorneys than criminal attorneys. And if you asked most of the very successful criminal defense attorneys in this country why they chose to go in that direction, you'd hear the same answer: When they went out on their own, nobody was there to teach them how to make it rain. They had to figure it out themselves.

The point of this book is to help you short-circuit the process.

Instead of having to discover over time that you should join relationship-based networking groups, show empathy to clients and referral sources, and respond to phone calls and emails immediately, this book will lay it out for you. You can learn it here rather than spending years figuring it out on your own.

IT TAKES GRIT

In the early 1990s, I worked for a law firm that handled criminal cases appointed to us by the county when the public defender couldn't represent a defendant due to a conflict of interest. We had seven or eight attorneys, and we were busy. But then the county began having financial problems, and we were no longer appointed to those cases. Overnight, most of our business disappeared.

I had been with the firm the longest. I was also the highest-paid attorney. So, I got fired.

I only had $4,000 in the bank and no one to help me. No choice; I had to figure out how to survive without someone else just giving me work.

What I had going for me was that over the years before I was fired, I had met the right people, both attorneys and judges, and I had a clear sense of what it would take to succeed on my own.

I quickly learned that friends will help you. If mine had any work they could send my way, they did. If it was criminal defense or something close to it, that I could handle, they sent it.

I also started doing special appearances for attorneys; if they were busy, I covered their court appearances. It helped me build strong relationships with the attorneys, which kept me getting the work. Lawyers get paid a per diem for special appearances. It wasn't much, but it kept me in court. I stayed visible, kept meeting prosecutors and judges, and remained in the mix.

Visibility was the key. I met the judges I needed to know and built lasting relationships, many of which I still have today.

My county created lists of attorneys eligible for court appointment and payment by the county for serious cases, like murder and three-strikes cases. If the public defender couldn't take the case and your name was on the list, you got the call from a court clerk who hoped you were available to come right over to court and accept the case. Because I had been around, built trust, had proven myself, and made a point of asking, I made it onto those lists.

For the first several years, most of my income came from court-appointed cases. I earned those cases through relationships and by consistently showing up soon after I got the call. I kept my expenses low and survived. At the same time, I started marketing, building a client base, and laying the groundwork for something more stable and long-term.

Things began to shift after about five or six years. People started being referred directly to me. They would say, "Bob, I want to hire you for this case." That's when I realized private clients were willing to pay far more than the county ever would. Working on just those court-appointed cases wasn't going to help me make a down payment on a nice home.

As private work increased, I took fewer court-appointed cases, and I was very gracious and appreciative when I let the court staff know I was not taking a case. The reason I started turning them down? I didn't want to become known to other attorneys and potential clients as the lawyer doing the same kinds of cases for the county at a fee that was a fraction of what the case was worth in private practice. I needed clients to know my hourly fee really reflected the value of my time. Eventually, I stopped taking those cases entirely. Then I was fully invested in my law firm and my ability to bring in cases.

It didn't happen overnight. It took three or four years after I lost my job. But I got there. And I wasn't part of any marketing groups or networking organizations. It was all word-of-mouth. I took lawyers to lunch, went to happy hours, and made myself visible. People got to know me, and once they trusted me not only to do good work but to treat their referrals well, they started sending clients.

That's one of the most important parts of building a practice. The people who refer to you have to trust that: 1) you will do a good job for the person they send, and 2) you will make them look good. The last thing they want is for a client to come back saying, "I never heard back from that guy you recommended."

I also learned how important it is to treat clients with empathy. Return their calls. Stay in touch. Imagine what they and their families are going through when charged with a serious crime. I'm old enough to remember when email wasn't even really a thing, and portable phones were anchored to bases next to the driver's seat.

Ignore a client, and they'll complain: "My lawyer never calls me back," or "They're too busy for me." You have to be in the mindset of staying in touch with your client, not only to understand the case and their point of view, but to show both the client and the referral source you care.

From the very beginning, I made it a rule to return calls as quickly as I could. Treat people with respect. Be decent. Show them you care. Starting out with only $4,000 in the bank, I didn't know any other way. This was how I believed you built a practice, and that's exactly what I did.

In criminal defense, there aren't many jobs at firms. Everyone knows the big national law firms, but they are almost all civil. Corporate cases. Lawsuits. The firm I worked for was the only criminal defense firm I knew of that hired attorneys. Everyone else was on their own.

After starting my own practice, I grew slowly over time. At different points, I hired an associate to work for me. There are just a few other criminal defense attorneys in the area who have an associate or a partner, and it is not like the large civil firms that hire dozens or even hundreds of lawyers. That structure just doesn't exist in criminal defense. You have to be able to make it on your own. I have handled criminal cases across the country, and it's the same everywhere.

No one taught me how to build my own practice. But the lessons I learned are transferable.

That does not mean you will make a million dollars your first year. It doesn't work that way. But if you stick with it and do the right things, it becomes very hard not to succeed.

THE UNEXPECTED RAINMAKER

I never imagined I'd write a book to teach attorneys about rainmaking.

Earlier in my career, I wanted to be known as a great trial lawyer. And I've tried a lot of cases and gotten good results. I know how to pick a jury best suited for the type of case and client, and nothing is more fun and satisfying than a closing argument. I feel like I'm very effective in trial. I never thought I would evolve into a rainmaker. That was never the plan, but sometimes that's how life goes.

When I was fired, I had to learn new skills. I could still focus on excelling in trial, but I also had to learn a completely new skill set, one I never expected to need. Hello, Rainmaker!

Back when I worked for a criminal defense firm, I was paid a salary. That number didn't change whether I brought the firm any cases. If I brought a case where the client wanted to hire me directly, I received ten percent of what the firm charged them. There really wasn't much of an incentive to get out there and hustle—the percentage was too low. At least when I was fired, I could keep 100 percent of what I quoted the client.

WHY I WROTE THIS BOOK

The idea for this book started during the pandemic. I saw large law firms across the country lay off hundreds, if not thousands, of lawyers. Many attorneys were suddenly out of work with no idea what to do next. I started getting resumes and emails from some. Most said something like, "If you have any work for me, I'd be grateful."

What struck me was how familiar their situation felt. They were unemployed, had little money saved, and were trying to figure out how to survive. It took me right back to when I got fired and had no direction. Well, this book will give you the roadmap, and it works.

What's more, I feel a duty to talk about empathy—not just for clients, but for fellow lawyers. How we treat each other in this profession matters more than people think.

This book isn't about making money as much as it's about creating freedom.

It's about working well with others, even when the stakes are high. In criminal defense, I get along very well with prosecutors, even when the client is facing life in prison.

I've tried several civil trials now where millions of dollars were at stake, and I've seen how poorly civil lawyers treat each other compared to prosecutors and criminal defense lawyers. Civil lawyers are much harder to deal with. The ones I've dealt with chase every possible angle, looking for tiny tactical advantages that, in the end, don't matter and cost their clients boatloads.

From a business standpoint, the other side's hostility makes no sense. A lawyer who refuses to give a simple extension or lies about what his client said in a deposition thinks he's gaining an edge. But when that same guy needs something from me, or eventually gets fired or laid off, and he's hoping someone like me might send him work, he's out of luck. Why would I ever refer a client to someone who treated me that way?

Empathy has been the secret to my business success in criminal defense, and I believe it can help civil lawyers, too. If more of them embraced it, they might enjoy their work more, it would make judges' lives easier, and perhaps they would avoid keeling over at their desks when they're sixty-seven. A little kindness goes a long way.

WHAT TO EXPECT

As you read, you will discover the importance of empathy and how to make it an integral part of your practice. You will learn more about the internal shifts you need to make for success, like stepping into the rainmaker role and mindset. You'll get step-by-step guidance on how to plan your so-called escape, build your practice from the ground up, and develop your list of clients and referral partners.

We'll dive deep into how to nurture your relationships to keep a steady flow of referrals, grow your client base from zero, and retain happy clients and referral sources for years to come. We'll talk about when and how to bring on support staff, and discuss why being a well-rounded business owner is vital to preventing burnout and truly feeling fulfilled. Finally, you will learn about planning for your retirement as a solo practitioner.

To make sure you stay organized, be sure to download the comprehensive checklist for starting your own law firm here: hartmannlawfirm.net/the-law-firm-startup-checklist/

Are you ready? Let's go.

CHAPTER 1

THE CASE FOR EMPATHY

I went to UCLA, then Loyola of Los Angeles Law School. I pretty quickly figured out I liked living near the beach in Orange County, which isn't cheap.

I was a political science major, and honestly, with that degree, there's not a whole lot you can do after school except become a lawyer or professor. So, I decided to go the law route.

One of my first jobs was as a deputy district attorney in the late 1980s. From there, I moved on to criminal defense and have been at it ever since.

But to be clear, it was never really my plan to become an attorney. At some point in college, I just thought, *You know what? Being a lawyer wouldn't be so bad.* I wasn't super passionate about it. But I figured it'd be a good career and could get me where I wanted to go.

My first job after law school was at a civil firm. We handled insurance defense representing insurance companies whose clients included corporations, homeowners' associations, and architects. If a fence broke at a condo and hurt someone, we defended the case.

I quickly realized I didn't like it. In civil law, you generally don't go to court very often. You're mostly sitting in your office doing things like depositions and interrogatories. As much as I enjoyed the partners and associates I worked with—and have stayed good friends with them over the years—the work, at least for me, was boring.

What I really wanted to do was be in the courtroom. That's where I felt I belonged.

On my second day as a prosecutor, I was in juvenile court in the middle of my first trial. The judge, who was the presiding judge for the whole court, asked me, "Mr. Hartmann, do you have any more questions for this witness?" And I said, "No, Your Honor. I think I've got it."

Now, that was rude. I didn't mean to be—it just came out the wrong way.

The judge looked at me, smiled, and said, "Are you sure?" It felt like there was a pause between each word.

"Yes, Your Honor. I'm sure."

Then the defense attorney stood up and said, "I have a motion to dismiss. Mr. Hartmann failed to prove one of the key elements of trespass." Opposing counsel was right. I had forgotten to ask the most important question a prosecutor should ask in a trespass case—and then, to make matters worse, I looked silly.

The judge turned to me and said, "Mr. Hartmann, this is a trespass case. You forgot to ask the officer whether the young man had permission to be there. That's a pretty critical element of trespass, don't you think?" I could have crawled under the counsel table. And he was right. For all the judge knew, the kid had permission to be there.

It was a huge lesson in humility. I was embarrassed, sure—but I also loved it. I knew right then, when the judge was good-naturedly giving me the business, that being a trial lawyer was what I wanted to do. It was fun. It was just me and the judge going back and forth. He was being nice to me, and in return, I was rude. The young man's lawyer was mad that the judge allowed me to reopen, and the young man was convicted anyway. It was a blast. That sealed the deal. I didn't want to be stuck behind a desk; I wanted to be in the courtroom.

More importantly, that day taught me two things: Never forget the critical elements of trespassing, and always show a little empathy—because one day *you* might be the rookie who forgets to ask the obvious question. The judge didn't bury me; he helped me. And that stuck.

Empathy in the courtroom doesn't look like a hug—sometimes it sounds like, "Are you *sure* you're done, counselor?" That experience shaped the lawyer I would become, and it's one of the reasons why empathy sits at the center of everything I do for my clients.

MOVING TO "THE DARK SIDE"

One reason I moved into criminal defense was that I had the opportunity to work with a very well-known lawyer in the community. Someone who handled a lot of high-profile cases. For a young guy like me, it sounded exciting.

The new job was a great fit too—more serious cases, and getting to do them more quickly than I would have been able to do as a prosecutor, and the chance to learn private practice. I had way too much confidence in my abilities. Confidence I hadn't earned yet. But I took the job.

And I'm glad I did. One of my new bosses taught me a lot about what it meant to be a lawyer. I also learned a lot from him about trial work. But even more than that, he taught me the importance of ethics, the value of my reputation, and how to be good with people. I saw how hard he worked at being successful.

He taught me things law school never did: how to *actually* be successful. My experience at the firm shaped who I am today.

Ironically, a couple of years later, they had to let me go because they didn't have enough business to keep me on. That's the law business.

EMPATHY AND ACCOUNTABILITY

Domestic violence cases are not exactly a popular topic. When I have a client with such a charge, I'll often advise them, "Look, while your case is pending, you should start an anger management class." I don't say it because I think they're guilty or to make them feel bad. I don't want them to think that I'm not doing everything I can because I know they did it. I say it because, at the end of the day, it often helps get them a better result. It shows the judge that the client is accountable and is taking the matter seriously.

And judges notice. They'll see my client is doing something proactively, not because they were ordered to, but because they chose to use this case as a way to better themselves. It makes a difference. When you advise a client to take those proactive steps on their own, they stand out, in a good way, among the defendants, to the judge and prosecutor. This is part of the secret sauce for getting good results on tough cases.

That said, it's not always easy to have such a conversation with a client. Some will say, "Won't that make me look guilty?" The answer is no. The jury will never hear about it if we go to trial. But the judge will know. And it often helps settle the case without jail. Can you think of any reason why the defense lawyer would not want his client to look good in front of the judge?

These are the little things that can positively change the outcome of a case. And it comes back to empathy. You have to be able to have that hard conversation with a client without making them defensive, while at the same time, conveying that you care and are on their side.

That's not easy to do. But it's one of the most important skills I've learned.

Empathy enables you to put yourself in your client's shoes and understand how they feel, given all the things going on in their lives, both legally and personally. Empathy guides what you say to a client and what to do to get the best result.

By the way, what is the best result? If a client committed the crime because of some underlying drug or alcohol problem, or because of a mental health problem, as crazy as it seems, the arrest and criminal charges are an opportunity for me to help them overcome a serious life problem, and in so doing, get a much better result in court. For me, that's the best result.

When the client presents their story to you, if you focus for a moment on what you can do to help them get better, most of the same principles will also help them receive a better sentence if the case is otherwise not defensible. And my experience is that the more you say and do this kind of thing, the more you start to exude empathy in your daily life.

WHY EMPATHY IS IMPERATIVE

Whenever I talk to a potential client, I always try to learn more about their personal life, their situation, and how they are invested in society—often a mitigating factor that might keep them out of jail.

These are important topics to uncover at the first meeting because it shows you care about them and understand what can happen to them if the case does not go well. This is where empathy begins.

What's more, you're taking the time to learn about them, show them why they should hire *you,* and convince them that *you* will do a great job for them. And this type of interaction helps your client understand why your hourly rate is higher than someone else down the street. You are sincere in your efforts to help because you care, and it's the extra time and effort that creates a great, rather than mediocre, result.

Let's say you have a client who is a respected police officer and he's charged with a DUI. Part of the job requires him to drive his police car. But he can't if his license is suspended. Put yourself in his shoes and in the moment. Try to understand how losing his license might cost the client his job and his home.

I had a case where the client had a driver's license certificate to haul nuclear waste. This certificate required that if he were ever convicted of a DUI, he would be banned from hauling nuclear waste. As a result, we had to figure out a way to keep his license from being suspended, even though the DMV had a really strong case against him. This client was married with kids, and his wife didn't work. I remember thinking to myself, the DMV didn't care if his license was suspended or if he became unemployed. But he and his family cared, and so did I.

Having empathy for his situation helped me communicate more effectively with him and the DMV. Having empathy creates a certain level of motivation to do well for your clients, even though it's not cost-effective for you. A lot of lawyers will only work the minimum necessary for the amount of money they were paid and won't do a nickel more. You go the extra mile because it's not only the right thing to do, you know it will pay off in the long run.

Immigration cases are another important place to show empathy. A client comes to you who has lived in the United States for twenty-five years; they're married, with kids who were born here. If they get convicted of a crime, there's a good chance they'll be deported, and the whole family's life will be forever disrupted. Having empathy means that when they call you and say they need your help to avoid a conviction, you have to do everything you can, within the ethics of the profession, and even think outside the box, to find solutions.

Or you have a client who is a doctor, who comes into your office for a case in which she's been indicted for cheating on her taxes. What the doctor truly wants to hear from you is that you care about her. You care about keeping her out of jail. You care that she will not have a felony on her record. You care about protecting her professional license. Once the client knows you care, the rest is downhill.

The good news is that once you begin to show empathy, it will inevitably become natural.

MY CASE FOR EMPATHY

In my experience, every judge wants to know why the client did what they did. And so, it's a question I ask every client. If I think they did it, I'll ask them why. And that's a key to getting the judge to give you a mitigated sentence. Knowing the answer to this question and being able to effectively communicate the "why" often results in a better sentence because, depending on the seriousness of the case, the judge finds your client accountable and remorseful.

Judges are human beings. If my mitigation brief conveys truthfulness, empathy, and a strong plan to get an otherwise lawful client back on track, the judge, more often than not, will take a chance on them with a lesser sentence.

HOW TO GET FIRED BY A CLIENT

Empathy leads to client retention. Conversely, when you lack empathy, you get fired. I often receive referrals from clients who have already hired a lawyer and desperately want to change. Often, it isn't that the attorney has done bad work; it's the way they treated the client. The most common complaint such clients have? Phone calls are not promptly returned, and if they are, the client feels their lawyer is rushing them off the call.

I've heard all sorts of examples of clients wanting to switch to me because their lawyer doesn't have empathy for them and their situation:

- The attorney doesn't care about me.
- It seems like they're too busy for me.
- They don't explain things to me.
- When we go to court, they just rush me out and don't explain what just happened.
- They talk "at" me, not "with" me.
- They send someone from their law firm to court. It's not the person I hired.

After listening to the initial complaints, I'll ask, "How much did you pay them?" I usually discover the lawyer's fee is too low.

One of the things you don't learn in law school is that you need to get paid sufficiently for the case you're working on, because if you don't, you will not put enough time into it to get the client a good result and make the referral source happy. Because of steep competition, many lawyers will not charge enough to reflect the time they should put into the case, so they don't get paid enough to represent the client well.

If you don't charge enough, then you have to bring in a lot more business to pay your bills. You will need to work on other things, which means you'll have less time to work on the case. It's also less likely you'll act empathetically if you didn't get paid enough. It's a vicious cycle.

Some clients feel powerless and resign themselves to the belief that's how all lawyers are. But other clients understand they are spending a lot of money and deserve better. That's usually when I get the call and hear their worries.

The way it goes down is interesting: The client finally gets sick and tired of the lack of attention, they call me and say," I want to hire you, but I'm a little shy. I don't want to fire the other lawyer. Would you fire her for me?" I can do it—it's one of those things that brings a little peace into the client's life, at a time when they really need it.

Here is the typical conversation:

The client says, "I'm going to fire the law firm. I'll hire you, Bob." Once I'm hired, I call the lawyer and say. "Your client, John Smith, is going to let you go. Could you send your client file right away and let me know how much money you've put into the case, because he wants some of it refunded." There are also some legal forms, called a Substitution of Attorney, that the prior lawyer may have to sign.

Unfortunately, many lawyers are unresponsive to the phone call, and the lack of empathy they showed the client earlier really becomes obvious at this stage. It's important to me to save the client from the drama of firing the lawyer.

Having empathy ties directly into your client's peace of mind, and it also benefits you because it gives the client more time to do those proactive things you need them to do to get a good result. He's not taking up mental space fretting about firing his lawyer. Instead, he is focused on work, on his life, and going to Alcoholics Anonymous classes, or doing whatever you need him to do to help you get a better result in his case.

A quick note: Attorneys should never try to steal clients from other lawyers. I wouldn't want people doing it to me. So, if a client says, "I'm thinking about getting rid of this lawyer, what do you think?" Normally, I'll advise them it's their decision. If you're looking at seven years in jail and your lawyer is not returning your phone calls, then you want to think about that in terms of how effective they are going to be for you when the time comes for them to really be your advocate. But if it sounds like the lawyer is doing a good job, and maybe not communicating enough, I'll advise the person to try informing the lawyer of that first, before switching to me.

GET TO KNOW YOUR CLIENT

When I begin getting to know a client, I ask them biographical questions before I get too much into their case. I'm going to need to learn a little bit about them before I can form judgments on what I can do to help them. I need to know if they're going to follow my advice, and selfishly, I want to know what they do for a living.

If I ask them what they do for a living and they say they deliver newspapers, I know they're not going to be able to afford me. I'd then ask whether they believe they have the funds for a private lawyer or would prefer a court-appointed lawyer, which won't cost them anything. If they choose the latter, then I'll tell them how to apply for a public defender. No matter what, I'll answer their questions and be respectful. By doing this little act, the referring attorney will know I took good care of their referral—so even if the referral doesn't work out, they'll be happy.

Biographical information also includes any professional licensing they have. If they're a doctor or lawyer, we need to know about that. If they're here on a visa and may be deported if convicted, we need to know that as well. We also need to know if they served in the military.

The next important question: What are the facts? Although I need to review police reports and conduct an investigation before I can give a client definitive advice about what to do, offer them a solution, or determine the best result for them. I generally have a pretty good idea of how the case will turn out after this portion of the meeting.

While lawyers are not permitted to guarantee or promise a particular result, I commit to doing my best for every client. Ninety-nine percent of the time, when the client comes in the door, I can tell whether or not they're going to go to jail. It comes with experience. If I can truthfully advise them that they most likely don't have to worry about jail, that helps them relax.

On the other hand, if jail is uncertain or likely, clients very much appreciate my being honest with them upfront, before collecting the fee. There are many alternatives to jail, such as house arrest, work programs, or community service. Oftentimes, more than the crime itself, the client's background becomes the critical piece in determining whether they spend time behind bars or in front of their television on house arrest.

You do not want to promise a good result, and only after getting the bad news, be forced to say "I'm sorry" to the client and family because you over-promised. You won't be at this job for very long, and you'll become a laughingstock. Our job is not only about doing good legal work. It's also about being truthful with clients while reducing their stress and anxiety about what's going to happen.

YOUR BOTTOM LINE

The most important thing to a client is that they feel their lawyer cares about what happens to them. They will be confident that you will do everything you can to help them. But in addition, the client will be much more likely to recommend you to others for legal services.

Anytime someone recommends you to a potential client, they put their own reputation on the line. Would you want to refer a client to an attorney who doesn't take the time to comfort the client, to convey that they will do everything they can to keep them out of jail? Common sense says "no." A key to being the go-to attorney is the ability to convey empathy to the potential client from day one.

Referrals are much more likely to come your way if you are a good listener and say the right things to the client. Certainly, your job performance for clients and referral sources is important. But even before you get a verdict, if the client has a good feeling that you sincerely care about the result, they will likely be willing to recommend you. This is true even if the result is not as good as you would have hoped. The fact that the client knows you tried your best and really understood what they were going through makes them and the referral source more tolerant of the result.

When attorneys go to court a lot, judges get to know them. And if a lawyer has a reputation for really caring about their client, versus just doing the minimum and getting out of there, in my experience, judges will be much more willing to listen.

The judge will place more trust in a client whose lawyer she knows to be empathic, hardworking, passionate, and has a good reputation. That extra trust might make the difference between a sentence of six months in jail and six months of community service.

Clients go into a courtroom and are generally intimidated and afraid of judges. They see in movies and on television that some judges are unpredictable. They worry whether the judge will like their lawyer. *Is he going to scream and yell at me or my lawyer?* When a client sees a judge treating their attorney respectfully, it means a great deal to them; it is impressive, gives them trust and confidence in the ultimate outcome, and reduces their stress and anxiety. Bingo!

Down the road, empathy translates into referrals. It helps deliver good results, is communicated to the referral source by the client, and is a key to becoming the rainmaker you want to be.

Now that you're an expert in empathy, it's time to start making some shifts in behavior and mindset that will set you up for success.

CHAPTER 2

THE RAINMAKER MINDSET

There is a critical mindset shift you must make before you embark on becoming your own boss. It all starts with *believing in yourself*. Do so, have a solid plan, follow it, and you will hit your goals.

Imagine you finally decide to leave your job—some of the partners have departed, and you see the writing on the wall for the firm's future. Or maybe it finally dawns on you that the partners will never accept you into their exclusive club. It could be that you don't like the work, or you're a new attorney and you haven't received a job offer you like. Maybe you're thinking you'd like to be in business within a year. Time will go by quickly. So now what? What steps must you take?

First, you've got to have confidence. You *can* make this kind of big move. There should be no doubt. Second, create a game plan. Start by asking yourself some key questions.

- Where am I going to set up my new office? Should I be near a courthouse or in a space with other lawyers who practice different types of law and can refer to each other? Is the spot I like easy to get to, and does it have easily accessible parking?
- How can I keep my expenses as low as possible? Is a nice office more impressive to potential clients, or are they happier if you're in a lesser office, showing you keep your fees to a minimum? What type of law library do I need? Should I incorporate? Should I hire a paralegal, a receptionist, or outsource to a virtual assistant? What about malpractice and office insurance?
- What will my marketing strategy look like? Should I join a networking group? What about different bar associations? How much time should I set aside every week for marketing? Who am I trying to drive to my website, what should it look like, and how much should I spend on it? Is search engine optimization worth it?
- Who do I need to connect with, and how do I do that? How do I meet lawyers who practice in different areas of law than I do? What about doing overflow work and special appearances for attorneys—how do I find them? Who at the courthouse runs the conflict panels that criminal defense attorneys can join to receive court appointments?

These questions are the outline of your plan. It's smart to start thinking through them six to twelve months before your target launch date. Write it all down. Seeing your plan in black and white does something powerful: It clarifies your thinking and boosts your motivation.

What about networking? Say you're working at a big firm or in the public defender's office and you've never really done much networking. Start now. Go to a networking event and see what it's like. You might be surprised at how approachable and helpful it all feels. You'll see people just like you—new to it, and then others who glide around the room and can easily talk to anyone. Once you realize you can do it too, your whole mindset starts to shift.

There are many groups to join, events to attend, and people to meet. Watching others successfully network is a real eye-opener. Although if you're like me and networking does not come naturally, once you engage in a couple of conversations, pass out a few cards, and relax, you'll find yourself thinking, *Wait, I can do this.* And that moment of realization? It cuts through the fear. It builds your confidence. And with that new confidence, you'll feel more inspired and more ready than ever to take the leap and get out of your bad situation.

FROM WORKER BEE TO RAINMAKER

Associates are essentially worker bees. They show up every day, and the partners assign them projects. Research this. Write that brief. Cover that appearance. Whatever the partner doesn't want to do is passed down the line.

At the time of hiring, the partners may encourage new associates to bring in some business. The associate might hear, "We'll give you a percentage of any case you bring in, but don't worry about it." That's the extent of the business development associates typically receive.

Networking and client acquisition aren't really emphasized to associates in most law firms. And certainly, law firms do next to nothing to teach rainmaking skills. That's because firms depend on them to do the work, and they don't want them to leave. The firm knows they'll leave once they realize, with some effort at rainmaking, they can make a lot more money outside of the firm than they are willing to pay them.

Partners expect associate attorneys to bill lots of hours—the more hours they bill, the more the partners split up at the end of the year, and perhaps they get a year-end bonus. At most law firms, associate attorneys are expected to bill around 1,800–2,000 hours a year. That's a lot of hours. And that's just what gets billed to the client. The truth is, they probably have to work even more than that, because not everything gets billed in full. Some of those hours get cut. The point is, billing is emphasized, not the associate learning what they need to know, so someday they can make the kind of money the partners do.

Most associates simply don't have enough time to go through the kind of training it takes to actually become a rainmaker. Honestly, I don't really understand why law firms have this mindset. On one hand, they're squeezing as much work out of associates as they can at the lowest cost. But by doing so, they're missing the chance to train those same associates to someday become a real financial asset to the firm, perhaps even an equity partner. Maybe the partners expect associates to just figure it out.

What I do know is that worker bees are in a job demanding constant output with very little downtime. They are not in an environment that supports growing as a networker or developing as a marketer. That's just not the world they're in.

When associates are hired into a civil law firm, there's usually some vague promise of a partnership track. Something like, "You'll start today, and if in seven years you're doing really well, we'll consider making you a partner." And that's about it. Some make it, most don't.

The reality? Most associates never become equity partners. What actually happens is that somewhere between years one and seven, they leave, get fired, or max out at senior associate or non-equity partner. By this time, they are making a decent salary, but their work product can be replaced by someone who makes substantially less. And once they're making more money than a second-year associate, since they're not bringing the firm any business, the partners don't care if they leave—they can replace them with someone cheaper.

The associate who has given so much to the firm over the years receives two weeks' notice, maybe some severance, and they're out. In fact, a recent report from the National Association for Law Placement found that in 2024, 74 percent of associates left their firms within just four years of being hired, which was up from a high of 72 percent the year prior.[1]

If associates are not prepared to leave, being let go can be devastating. Financially, it might be hard just to make next month's mortgage payment. And, the lawyer usually doesn't have the rainmaking skills they need to bring in their own business—they are dependent on working on cases brought in by others.

Even if an associate tries a lateral move to another law firm, they typically don't have the resume to walk into the interview and say, "Here's why you should start me at a higher salary. Here's why I belong on your partnership track. I will make you a lot of money." Most associates just don't have those skills. Be honest with yourself—do you?

LEVELING UP

If you're unhappy where you are, and you've thought about starting your own practice, or find yourself on the outside looking in at your old firm, you must commit to learning the necessary rainmaking skills.

And it's not easy in today's world. Just look at how much is on an associate's plate. They're slammed at work, billing like crazy.

---

1 Debra Cassens Weiss, "Attrition rate is 'markedly higher' for associates of color, NALP Foundation says," *ABA Journal*, April 29, 2025, https://www.abajournal.com/news/article/attrition-rate-is-markedly-higher-for-associates-of-color-nalp-foundation-says

And on top of that, they're busy at home. They might have kids in sports or dance. They're married. They have friends.

If you are that associate, you know that it's tough to find the time or even the mental space to think about shifting your mindset. Even if the idea of implementing a true change crosses your mind, the thought can be daunting.

In my experience, you have to decide: *I want to learn how to be a rainmaker.* Whether you're planning to leave your firm now, next year, or five years from now doesn't matter. What is important is that you start learning the needed skill sets now. Because if you ever do get fired, at least being somewhat prepared to be on your own softens the blow. You might even find yourself thinking, *Well, here's my chance to finally become a millionaire.*

You also have to commit to learn. And if you're like me, you'll want to quickly learn the things you really need to know about being in business on your own.

Start by looking around your firm. Chances are, there are one or two partners who bring in the bulk of the business. Ask yourself: *What do they do that makes it possible?* Most associates think, *Well, they've just had those clients for years. They automatically send them business.* But ask yourself, *why?* Why is the referral source still sending work to the partner, even when some cases likely didn't turn out well?

Here's my hunch: It's because when the referral source calls, the partner picks up. When they send an email, it is promptly answered. When there's a new matter needing urgent attention, the partner is on it. That kind of responsiveness might not even be seen by most associates. I believe this is true at most firms, even for the largest. It's usually just a handful of partners bringing in most of the firm's business.

So, if I were an associate, I'd want to take one of those rainmaking partners out to lunch and ask how they have kept the referral source for ten or fifteen years, given that not every outcome is perfect. But how many associates actually make this effort? Who has the nerve to ask those types of questions? Probably none. It's intimidating. You feel like you can't just ask the senior partner to lunch; it feels awkward, like you're admitting you don't know anything.

The reality is, when you're deep in the grind, just turning out work every day, and then going home to your family, it's hard to break out of the cycle and think long-term. You have to make a conscious decision: I'm doing it. I'm going to learn how to be a rainmaker because I have a bigger career plan. Think about whether it's five, ten, or fifteen years down the road, you want to run your own shop or be a high-earning partner at a big firm. Either way, you'll need more than what law school taught you and more than what most law firms teach you.

Let's be honest: We learned nothing in law school about how to bring in business.

We learned torts. We learned about offer acceptance and consideration. We didn't learn how to treat potential clients and referral sources. We didn't learn how to network. So, if you've made the big decision, you want to change, you want to become a rainmaker, just know, there's not a lot of guidance out there. There was no playbook until now.

How do you start? By learning rainmaker skills before you quit or get fired. Look at the personalities of the rainmaking partners. Watch how they interact with people outside the firm: clients, potential clients, even other lawyers. Why do people keep referring business to them? Sit down and think it through. My guess? Most of the time, it comes down to one thing: empathy.

Empathy shows up in all those small ways. Promptly returning phone calls, not making clients wait a day for an email reply, being concerned, and talking on a Saturday. These things really matter. They mean so much to clients who depend on their attorney for everything. That's the first thing a lawyer who wants to be a rainmaker has to understand.

Some lawyers try joining networking groups. But I've seen a lot of attorneys fail in those settings. Why? Because they bring their law firm persona into the group. Networking groups only work if people know what you do and trust you enough to refer business. But if you're never available, always "too busy" to meet with the group, how are they supposed to get to know you?

NETWORKING LIKE A RAINMAKER

If you decide to join a networking group, you must do what it takes to be successful in that chapter. It's more than just showing up to the weekly meetings. You have to take the time to learn the business needs of the other people in the group, sit down for an hour with each member to learn what they do and how you can help them, and even visit other chapters of the group in your area so you can meet the best potential referral sources. Most importantly, connect with people. Begin genuine business relationships.

And here's a key to success: It's not about talking about yourself. It's all about them. It's about letting them talk about themselves.

What you don't want is to come off as the person in the group who only talks about their own business or is just there hoping for referrals. It never works. It has to go both ways. You're building relationships. You're building trust. Unless you take an interest in referring to others in your group, you're not going to get much out of it.

For example, I have a networking partner who is a notary. It's the same for an investigator, financial planner, CPA, florist, website designer, or even a therapist. And if anyone in my world needs any of the services offered by our group's members, I'm pretty aggressive about connecting them. Nothing enhances your credibility in networking and creates more referrals for you than making great referrals to others.

This is where empathy really comes into play. You have to be willing to show people you're more concerned about referring business to them than they are about referring business to you. You have to be able to clearly convey this mindset.

How do you do that? Well, what I do, even when I'm busy, is make the time. I'll set aside an hour, sometimes even an hour and a half, to meet with someone from my networking group. Just the two of us—over coffee, lunch, a cocktail, or miniature golf. Not over the computer.

When we meet, I make a point of talking about them first. I'll ask about their family in a nice, respectful way. "Tell me about your why? What drives you? What are you passionate about?" Then I'll ask about their practice. "What kind of clients are you looking for?" "Who do you want to meet?" "Is there anyone I can introduce you to in my office?"

And then I think about my own network. *Is there someone I know who might be a good match or a good connection for this person?* I always let them go first. I want them to feel heard. I want them to know I'm not there to pitch to them or ask for anything. I'm there to help. I don't want to come across as selfish or needy. And that approach has worked for me like nothing else.

Now, in the first few moments after meeting someone new, I'll ask myself whether there is someone I can introduce them to who can help them. It's become second nature. To give you an example: I recently met a trust attorney from a different networking group, and asked her, "Would you like to be introduced to someone who works in the funeral planning industry?" She said yes, so I made the introduction. It took all of five minutes. Doing little things like that is a great way to grow a group of people who will refer back to you.

One of the things people told me when I was younger was: "Go to bar association events. Network. Make connections. You'll meet other lawyers there." But honestly? I found them to be useless as a means of generating clients. When you're in a room with as many as 700 people at a bar association gala, it's really hard to do anything more than exchange a few words with someone. Maybe you get a little spark of connection and agree to meet later, but for the most part, it feels like a waste of time. There are so many lawyers who do what you do in that group, it's hard to gain any traction. It's too loud, too busy, too surface-level.

What I found to be much more effective is something much simpler. If I run into someone and think that it's someone I'd like to get to know better, I'll just say, "Listen, how about we grab a cup of coffee sometime? I'd love to hear more about your practice." That's it.

Same thing in a networking group. Let's say you're in a group with fifty people, and they're all there for the same reason: to make business connections. What I do for each person I want to meet is go up to each person individually and say something like, "Hey, I heard you're an immigration attorney. I'd love to get to know more about your practice. A lot of my clients have immigration issues; maybe there's a way we can work together." Then we pull out our calendars, make a plan, and meet for coffee.

It's not awkward because we're all there for the same reason—to meet people and set up those types of meetings.

Not only does this start the process of building a referral partner, but more often than not, I've made a new friend. And the benefit isn't just professional, it's personal. I don't think we talk about that enough.

For example, in one of my networking groups, I did exactly that, and I ended up forming a core group of six or seven friends. Not just colleagues, but friends. I travel with them. They've become some of my best friends. And none of that would've happened if I hadn't taken the time to get to know them on a personal level. Some of them aren't even lawyers. I just genuinely wanted to understand what they do and how I might be able to help.

I'd ask, "Is there anything I can do for you? I've got a great network. Can I introduce you to someone who might be a good connection for you?" And when you ask people that, especially in a way that's truly not selfish, when you let them talk first, their eyes light up. Every time. Be the person with the great connections you're willing to share.

OVERCOMING THE FEAR OF FAILURE

Putting yourself out there can be intimidating, but you have to reject the fear of failure. You have to completely let go of fear. You can't be afraid of failing. And not only that, but you also have to get over the fear of speaking—person to person and in front of groups.

When you have an opportunity to talk to someone, whether it's in front of your networking group, a stranger you just met at court, or even a friend, you need to be able to say, in five or ten words, why you'd like to connect. What is it about the person you want to learn?

And sometimes, the other person is going to say they're too busy. What they really mean is, "I'm too busy to meet with you." That's fine; it's their loss. There are plenty of lawyers out there who can be great referral sources for you. You *will* find them.

Once you really understand that, the fear starts to shrink. You start building confidence.

When I went out on my own, I didn't figure it out right away. I got rejected a lot. But I had to stop worrying about people saying no. Because most of the time, when someone says no, they're not going to be mean about it. They'll just say, "You know what, I'm slammed right now," or, "My schedule's full for the next couple of months." You get the hint. And then you move on.

It's like dating. You don't get hung up on one person who isn't interested. There are a million other fish out there, and any one of them at any time can refer a great case to you.

One time, I went to a conference where a nationally known lawyer was hosting a breakout session. His work was probably one of the key reasons the defense won a high-profile case, and I thought I shouldn't pass up on an opportunity to meet him. So, I sat through the presentation, waited until the room cleared, and approached him while he was packing up at the podium. I said, "Hi, I'm Bob Hartmann, a sole practitioner from Orange County. I followed you during your big trial and thought you were incredibly effective. I'd love to grab a cup of coffee with you if you're available."

He replied, very politely, "I would love to, but my schedule is just too full. I can't make it happen."

Rejection! And yeah, I was a little disappointed, because I really admired his skills as a trial lawyer. But he didn't want to meet. He was likely thinking, *Who is this guy?* He didn't need to give me his time.

Still, that rejection didn't throw me off. Just a little bump. The sting ws over in seconds. The next day at the conference, I bumped into someone else who became a great new connection.

BUILDING YOUR CREDENTIALS

To truly level up, I also recommend improving your credentials as much as you can. For example, in California, the State Bar offers the title "certified legal specialist." It requires passing a certification exam in a specific area of law, recommendations from judges and lawyers familiar with your work, and significantly more continuing education than other attorneys take. You must re-certify every five years. If the Bar approves your application, you're recognized as a certified specialist in that area of law. It's a title that makes you stand out from the other lawyers who do what you do, and referral sources will tell people about your specialization when they send you new clients.

Take criminal law, for example. In the entire state of California, there are over 160,000 lawyers, and as of 2025, only around 400 are certified specialists in criminal law, and I'm one of them.

Having the credential gives me greater confidence when identifying and engaging with potential referral sources. When people talk to me, they see I've earned something additional. The "certified specialist" next to my name tells them I've met a higher standard. It helps them trust that my advice is correct.

Other ways to level up? Teach—become an adjunct professor at a local law school, or use your expertise and speak at legal conferences. To others, this shows your knowledge and experience in those areas of the law, and you'd be surprised at how many students you will run into around town over the years.

If you want to be seen as a leader in your field, leveling up your professional standing wherever you can is key.

DRESS THE PART

We all know first appearances are critical, so it's important to dress well in court and when networking. A great suit, tie, and shoes inspire confidence and trust not just in your client. When you look successful, it translates to others who interact with you.

And it works both ways. When I know I look good, I feel more confident. I'm more likely to walk up to someone and say, "Hey, want to grab a cup of coffee?"

Ironically, the way a lawyer dresses can sometimes lead to unintended consequences.

After a trial, I generally talk to the jury. After they have given the verdict, the judge usually tells them, "If you want to stick around and talk to the lawyers, I'm sure they'd love to hear your thoughts about the case."

Once, when speaking to a juror, she said something that totally surprised me. "You had the absolute worst case ever. It was very clear that your client did it. He confessed. Why did you even go to trial?" She said, "It was eleven to one for guilt in the first ten minutes of deliberations, and the last juror voted guilty after about an hour." I was starting to think about a fast exit, but then she continued, "You know what? I really loved your ties."

I stopped and said, "Wait, what? You paid attention to that?"

She said, "Oh, absolutely. I paid attention to your shoes and your ties. I even noticed how the D.A. dressed. And honestly, some days? Not great."

She also added that a couple of other jurors talked about one of my ties. Then she told me, "If there was any way we could've voted for your client, we might have, just because you had so much more presence, from how you looked that one day."

I'm pretty sure the juror was telling the truth. A crazy compliment for sure, but an unusual learning experience. So that's what jurors think about! Your clothes, your confidence, your presence, not so much the evidence, make a difference sometimes!

BUILDING YOUR FINANCIAL FOUNDATION

There's a common rule of thumb: When you start your own business, you want to have six months worth of living expenses in the bank. If you don't make a nickel for six months, you can still pay your mortgage, your kids' school, your car payment, whatever you need to stay afloat. That's why leaving your job isn't something you do overnight. You need to start setting money aside early so when the time comes, you can leave with confidence.

If you know you're covered financially, it takes a huge weight off your shoulders as you begin your new practice. It lowers your stress and anxiety, and it gives you the freedom to focus on bringing in the right cases, not just whatever comes through the door because you're desperate. You won't feel forced to take on a client you know you shouldn't.

Most attorneys know within the first three or four months of working at a firm whether they want to stay there. So, setting a goal to leave a job in a year should give you enough time to bank some money and get ready. If that's you, start preparing now.

Make sure you have enough money in the bank. And when you announce your new firm is opening on October 1st, open on October 1st. Not a day later. Everyone should know your timeline. You need to be ready. Send out announcements, throw a party, and invite everyone you know. Get the word out! Have a lot of people there—friends, family, and other future referral sources.

Of course, not everyone gets to leave on their own terms. Some lawyers get fired. And if that happens, one thing you can try to do is negotiate a severance. As an employer, I might offer a severance to deflect potential lawsuits and complaints down the line.

Even if you receive something as they push you out, what you do after being fired depends a lot on how prepared you were. If you've been marketing yourself and networking consistently, then you already know what to do.

You already have a contact list, a strategy, and people who know who you are. When the time comes, you just let people know, "Hey, I'm leaving the firm, and starting in four weeks, this is what I'll be doing, and I'd appreciate your support." You don't have to say you were fired. Just say you're moving on. And because you've already laid the foundation, you can move fast.

But if you're fired and you haven't done any networking or marketing, it's tougher.

If you're an associate at a law firm and you want to become an equity partner, you have to learn how to bring in business. Your first year or two as a lawyer can be dedicated to learning "how to be a lawyer." After that, your focus should shift to being the best lawyer you can be *and* networking.

If you're an associate at a big firm and you're doing great, that's awesome. But even then, start figuring out how to bring in work. Most firms will give you a bonus, and if and when you bring in enough, they'll make you an equity partner. Truthfully, as an associate, you should be networking and bringing in some business.

Because if something bad happens, the firm implodes, you'll be ready. Your network will be in place. You'll be able to send a few emails, make a few calls, and let people know, "I'm on my own now." And you'll be amazed at how many people want to help you. Really! You'll be surprised by how many lawyers will go out of their way to send you referrals, especially in those first six months. They know what it's like, and they want to help.

But if you haven't laid the groundwork, if you've done no marketing, saved no money, built no network, you could end up like a lot of lawyers did during the pandemic. They got laid off, had nothing saved, had a lot of debt, and had to move back in with their parents.

The lesson is simple: Always be networking, always be marketing, and always be prepared.

If you do well enough, maybe you'll become an equity partner. But if bad news hits, it's not a disaster. It doesn't have to be the end of the world. The good news is, you will be ready.

What else do you need to know to get started? Let's explore other considerations in the next chapter.

CHAPTER 3

PLANNING YOUR TRANSITION FROM EMPLOYEE TO OWNER

Picture this: You wake up one morning and realize you're never going to make partner at your law firm, and honestly, you're not even sure you want to. But you're married. You have a mortgage. You have kids. And your lifestyle is expensive. You feel stuck in a rut.

A lot of lawyers arrive at this moment. So, the question they should ask themselves is, *Am I going to waste my prime earning years here, making others a lot of money, or am I going to be a little bolder and do something to make my mark?*

An important step in bettering your life is deciding you're ready to explore leaving. That's it. You don't have to quit tomorrow. You just need to start seriously thinking about what it looks like to own your own firm. One way to do so is to make a simple list of the pros and cons.

Let's say the pros of staying at your current firm look something like this:

- It's stable employment.
- I make enough to cover everything.
- I can afford a vacation once a year.
- I drive a nice car.

Stability and guaranteed income—there's nothing wrong with that.

Let's look at the other side of the coin, the cons of staying:

- I will never become an equity partner.
- I will always depend on someone else for my income.
- They bill me out at $500/hour, most of which the partners split.
- I'm never going to achieve the vision I had when I became a lawyer.

That vision might include:

- Setting my own schedule
- Taking great vacations whenever I want
- Driving my dream car

- Living in the kind of house and in the neighborhood I've always wanted
- Having financial independence now and passing it on to my children
- Experiencing real professional satisfaction
- Being able to come and go at the office as I please

Once you've created your list, take your time before making any final decisions. This is not something you figure out in a day. Talk to your spouse or partner. Talk to your financial advisor. Talk to friends and attorneys you think might become referral sources. Think through what this would mean for your life and your family.

You also need to ask yourself: *Can my family survive financially if my income drops for a while? Can I set aside six to nine months of expenses so I can give myself time to transition, even if I don't make much at the start?*

And the most important question is:
Do I believe in myself enough to pull this off?

Because at the end of the day, it's about choosing to be bold. It's about deciding that you and your family's happiness matter, and you're ready to take the next step to build a life where *you,* not the partner in the corner office, are in control.

AVOID THE MISTAKES

Oftentimes, attorneys who decide to go out on their own miss some of the crucial steps for success. They pick a date, move into their new office, and say, "Okay, let's start." Then they realize no cases are coming in, and they have no real prospects. Clients don't just appear because you hang out a shingle.

Preparation is king, right? Most lawyers don't know what the actual steps are to build a practice. I wouldn't have known about the value of relationship networking if someone hadn't told me. A lot of newly solo attorneys think that just sending a letter to all their friends, family, and old clients (which can be problematic if leaving a firm) is enough to get things rolling. And while it's a start, it usually means your client base grows very slowly, given the limited circle of people.

But because you're reading this book, you are on the fast track.

TELLING YOUR COLLEAGUES AND YOUR GREATER NETWORK

Once you've decided to go out on your own and set a date for leaving, it's time to start letting people in your world know what your plans are. But be careful who you tell. The people you share this with need to be trustworthy enough to keep it to themselves. It's very important they don't let the news slip before you've had the chance to tell your employer.

If you don't fully trust your colleagues to keep it in the vault, then don't tell them. Simple as that.

Speaking as someone who owns a law firm, if I found out one of my associates was planning to leave before they told me, I'd start to wonder: *Are they still fully focused? Are they giving the same effort to the work I assign them, or are they already halfway out the door, using work hours to job hunt or make exit plans? Are they going to try to steal my hard-earned clients? What about my intellectual property—the systems and processes I've put in place? They're getting ready to leave on my dime!*

For me, the day I confirmed an associate intended to leave would also be their last day at my firm. I'd require them to clear out their office and be escorted out by building security the same day. I suspect most firms would do the same.

When the time does come to share your decision with trusted colleagues, it doesn't have to be a big formal announcement. It can happen casually, maybe over lunch or drinks. Just let them know, "I've decided to leave the firm. I'm at a point in my career where I'm making a lot of money for the firm, and I'd rather keep it. I have the ability to bring in clients and do great work for them, and it's time." Don't be afraid to admit you're a little nervous about it. Let them know you're counting on their support.

One important thing to remember when you start sharing your plans: Do not badmouth your current firm. It might be tough, especially if they underpay you, or the way the firm is run is part of why you're leaving. But keep those thoughts to yourself. It's a good habit to get into. Why? Because complaining within the legal community has a way of coming back around. The partner you're tempted to complain about? They might end up being a judge a few years down the line. And one day, you might find yourself standing in front of them, arguing a big case. You don't want to be the person who burned that bridge.

TELLING THE BOSS

When you graduate from law school, you know the law, but you have no idea how to actually be a lawyer. You don't know how to run a practice, write a proper brief, make a court appearance, speak to a judge, market yourself, or build a network.

Your first employer is usually the person who gives you the opportunity to learn some of those things. You're learning how to be a lawyer while they pay you. It's important to remember when it's time to move on.

When you're ready to resign, you will likely dread the conversation, but it needs to be professionally handled. Don't just barge into your boss's office and drop the news. Make an appointment with their assistant. Be respectful of their time, and no matter how unhappy you are, keep in mind they've helped you move your career forward on some level.

I'd start the conversation like this:

"I have some news, it's important, and I wanted you to be the first to know."

Your goal in this conversation is to make the partner feel respected. Make them feel like they've played a meaningful role in your growth, and at the same time, remember the marketing guru in you: The goal is to maintain a long-term professional relationship with the firm.

When you say, “I’ve made the decision to go out on my own,” follow it up with something like: “I’m only able to do this because of everything I’ve learned here. I’m so appreciative of the training, the experience, and the chance to learn from your team. The firm helped me become the lawyer I am today.”

And if it’s true, you also want to make it clear you’re not going to compete for the same clients. Reassure them you’re opening a solo practice, and their clients aren’t your target. Let them know you’d never try to poach anyone, staff or client, and you’ll always speak highly of your experience at the firm.

Say things like:

“I’m really thankful for the opportunity you’ve given me.”

“If I ever have a chance to send work your way, I will, because I appreciate the people here.”

Frame the whole conversation as a positive. Show your gratitude. Be respectful. They gave you your start, and you wouldn’t be where you are without them.

When you give notice, let them know you’re happy to keep working for a couple of weeks while they find someone to take your place. Doing so gives you time to put the finishing touches on building your new practice and allows you to set a start date for your new office. Or they may say, "We no longer need you; clear out your desk." Prepare yourself for either outcome.

It's okay to close the conversation by saying something like: "If we ever have the opportunity to refer to each other, I'd really appreciate it." Letting your employer know you're leaving should be an uplifting moment, not a confrontation.

I went through that experience at my first job at the insurance defense firm.

You know how life turns on a dime? One day, a friend from law school called. He was a deputy district attorney and was moving out of state. The office told him that if he knew anyone who wanted the job, he should reach out. He called me and said, "Bob, I know you want to be a D.A."

I interviewed, got the job, and then had to sit down with the partner at my firm. I said, "As you probably know, given all the red marks the partners put on my work, I don't enjoy this kind of law. I want to be in court, doing trials, not sitting behind a desk. It's just not my style."

Because we got along personally so well, the partner felt comfortable telling me he had noticed it seemed that wasn't the type of law I wanted to practice, and he was glad he wouldn't have to be the one to let me go. We started laughing. It was actually a great moment. The fact that we could have such an honest, lighthearted exchange was a blessing. I've stayed friends with the partners at the firm for nearly forty years, and they are kind enough to allow me to handle their criminal referrals.

The point is, it's so important to be honest and appreciative. You never know how life will unfold. There's no need to make enemies. The legal community isn't big; your reputation is everything, and it follows you. When you leave a firm, you want to be remembered as someone who handled it with class and integrity, and in the long run, someone to whom they would like to send business.

Remember, even if you are fired, it's almost always not personal—they may have lost a big client, have financial issues, or whatever it may be. You want the attorneys to always think of you as a person they trust to refer cases.

GENERATE EXCITEMENT

After giving notice, it's important to finalize the official date you'll open the doors to your own firm. And once it's in place, you want to create some buzz—make it a great launch party. Host an event in your new office and invite everybody you know. Friends, colleagues, former clients, other attorneys, judges, everyone! It's a chance to show off your new space and let people know you're open for business. Pass out something in writing, highlighting the type of work you'll be doing. Have plenty of business cards ready to pass out, and make sure you collect cards from your guests as well. They all get thank-you notes and are added to your network.

I recently went to an office opening where the lawyer did exactly that. The event was short, just about an hour, but it was packed. The firm owner invited representatives from the city, who showed up with a certificate to officially welcome the practice to the Chamber of Commerce. A state senator even came by to offer congratulations.

At least 100 people were there, and the message was clear: This lawyer knows what they're doing. When people see that kind of turnout and recognition, it sends a powerful signal. It builds credibility. It creates visibility. It makes people think, this attorney is the real deal.

> **Events like that don't just celebrate the launch. They position you as someone who's already part of the professional community and someone worth paying attention to.**

By the way, how should you exchange cards? When you receive their card, don't immediately put it away. Spend a moment carefully looking at it—the person who handed it to you will appreciate you because they know you're thinking about how you can refer work to them.

OUTLINE YOUR GOALS FOR DAY ONE

To be honest, I'm not the kind of person who makes lists. But when you're getting ready to launch your own firm, I highly recommend creating an outline with specific, actionable steps to help make your opening as effective as possible.

Even before you give notice at your current firm, start preparing. There are a lot of moving parts, and you'll want to have a plan in place so nothing is missed.

Here are some things to start thinking about:

- You'll need a website and maybe a logo.
- You'll need business cards and stationery.
- You're going to want to join a networking group and start building up your own network.

Explore networking groups, and really look carefully at them; it's important not to just pick the first one you hear about. Visit three or four different groups and see which is the best fit. How do you know if the networking group will work for you? Are there lawyers from different practice areas and other individuals who are willing to refer to you, and are you willing to do the same for them?

Outside of your networking group, start meeting with lawyers you already know. Take them out for lunch, or meet them for a glass of wine. There's nothing better than one-on-one time when you're building connections. Let them know your timeline. Say something like, "Six months from tomorrow, I'm opening my own firm." Ask them to think about you when they want to refer business, and you'll do the same.

Just remember: Networking is not a one-way street. You're not there to talk for an hour about how they can send you clients. Show a genuine interest in their firm. Ask how *you* can help *them*. Because the truth is, the more you give to them, the more they will try to give to you. It's human nature. Send nothing, receive nothing. Your goal is to develop your own network full of people you think of, and who think of you, whenever a legal issue comes up.

There are other key things to take care of as well.

- Open new bank accounts for the business. Be sure you know the rules regarding law firm trusts in your state. If they're anything like California, they require a lot of attention.
- Set up office and liability insurance.
- Get serious about staying organized. Use a law firm management and calendaring system you can trust. You won't be able to remember everything, and you shouldn't try.

BANK ACCOUNTS

When starting your law practice, you will need to open a minimum of two bank accounts. First, you'll need a business checking or operating account. Next, you'll need one or more client trust accounts to hold client funds. Be sure to check your state's requirements. [2]

---

2 "Opening Bank Accounts for Your Law Firm," *Law Firm Basics*, accessed September 18, 2025, https://lawfirmbasics.com/law-firm-bank-accounts/

OFFICE SPACE

Let's talk about office space. Personally, I don't think working from home is the best idea. You don't need a massive office or the most beautiful suite on the best street downtown. But you do want a clean, professional-looking office, easy for clients to find, with good parking. Make it simple for them to come see you; an office way off the main road, which requires a bunch of different turns, is not as good as something easy to get to. Expensive parking without a validation is also a no-no. Clients care about how easy it is to get to your office and whether you cover the parking.

You'll also want to think about your office setup. Do you want to be completely on your own, or do you want to work alongside other attorneys? If you decide to share space, think about who you want around you. Are they in different practice areas than you? The choice can make a big difference in the quantity and quality of referrals you receive from your office-mates.

INSURING YOUR BUSINESS

It's important to note there's a difference between office and malpractice insurance.

Office insurance is what covers you if your computer is stolen, your copy machine walks off, or if someone slips and falls in your office. You definitely want to have it. You don't want a messenger coming into your office, slipping on a tear in the carpet you somehow missed, fracturing their back, and suing you, only to find out you're not covered. That's a nightmare. So yes, you absolutely need office insurance. No question.

Shop it though, and get your best rate. It's likely someone in your networking group offers this type of insurance. And although you're spending money with them, it's a way for you to meet another professional, learn more about what they do, and create a back-and-forth referral relationship.

Malpractice insurance, what we call errors and omissions insurance (E&O), is a whole different thing. It protects you if you make a professional mistake and harm a client. And, as with any insurance, there are different levels of coverage. I carry a policy that covers up to $1 million per claim and $3 million aggregate, because I handle cases where the stakes are high.

Thankfully, I've never had to make a claim on it. But even if you never file a claim, it's critical, and it helps you sleep at night if you have a problem with a client or worry you made a mistake. In California, attorneys are legally required to disclose if they don't carry E&O coverage. Clients have to sign off and acknowledge that they know you don't carry it. Think that inspires confidence or trust in a client or referral source? Of course not. Bite the bullet, do the right thing, buy it to protect you and your client. Once again, many networking groups will have someone in the group who is more than willing to sell you a policy and get to know what you do.

For criminal defense, E&O insurance actually isn't extremely costly because you don't have many critical deadlines. If I miss a date or deadline for a brief, the court may just give me a new date.

The client's not going to jail due to a lawyer's mistake. However, in areas like personal injury, employment law, and workers' compensation cases, if you miss a deadline, that could be it. You might be out of court. Those are high-risk practice areas, and the malpractice insurance for those lawyers is absolutely critical.

Attorneys walking around town without insurance are dangerous. While it's tempting for an attorney new to their own practice to try to save a few bucks, E&O is not the place to do so.

So, take the time *now* to consider your plans. Set a clear start date. Create a list of tasks. Set goals around what needs to happen next. Talk to friends and colleagues already out on their own. Planning and preparation set you up for success.

CHAPTER 4

BUILDING YOUR PRACTICE

As I mentioned earlier, Merriam-Webster defines a *rainmaker* as "a person who brings in new business; also, a person whose influence can initiate progress or ensure success."

As the rainmaker of your own firm, I recommend you strive to be both. You need to be someone who brings in business *and* someone who drives success, by your own hand and by helping others around you rise.

This means being comfortable talking about money. It means looking a potential client in the eye and saying, "Here's what I can do to help you, and here is what it will cost." It means making genuine connections not only with clients, but also with referral partners.

There are really two parts to being a good rainmaker. First, you need to develop the necessary skill set if you don't already have it. For clients, it includes connecting with them through empathy, constant follow-up, and delivering great results. For referral sources, it's about building business relationships, maintaining consistent touchpoints, and making them look good to the clients they send your way. But second, and here's where you'll get to another level, you want to be able to teach someone else to do it, too.

A NEW ASSOCIATE

As your firm grows, you'll face a choice. Either turn away cases because you're too busy, or bring someone on to help. Here, we're talking about whether to bring on an associate attorney.

There's a lot that goes into hiring an associate, even glossing over all the employment issues. They have to fit your culture and be trained to do everything the way you want it done. Then you have to hope they do a good job with the clients, so the referral sources remain happy.

At first, they'll handle the overflow. But if you train them well, maybe over time, they'll begin to generate their own business. Maybe they start paying their own salary. Maybe they even bring in new clients for the firm. That's when you really start to maximize your rainmaking ability because now someone else is adding to your bottom line.

You can set up a system where, for the cases they bring in, they get a percentage of the fees, which should reflect that you are carrying all the overhead and assuming all the risk. It's a smart way to grow your practice. That's how you build something sustainable. That's how you build wealth.

Some people worry, "What happens if the associate becomes a great rainmaker and decides to go out on their own?" My answer is simple: That's okay. You part as friends. You've been their mentor. You helped each other grow. And in most cases, the mutual respect lasts.

So, if you train someone and they leave after four or five years to start their own firm, great. You benefited from their work product and the fees they brought in while they were with you. You can bring in someone new and teach them, too. And now you've got a lasting referral relationship with someone who sees you as their mentor. That kind of respect doesn't go away.

We've already talked about networking, marketing, relationships, and how empathy sits at the heart of it all. But becoming a rainmaker doesn't happen overnight. It's a layered process. It takes time. You build it brick by brick, kind of like John Wooden's Pyramid of Success. You start with a foundation.

Here are a few of those building blocks:

- Do high-quality legal work
- Deliver outstanding client service with empathy

- Build a strong reputation within the legal community
- Treat clients and referral sources well

No matter why you left your job, it's going to take time to build all of this, but it *will* come.

Here's another scenario where you'll be tempted to bring in an attorney. Maybe after a year or so on your own, you're doing fine. But a case walks through the door, and you think, *I just don't want this one.* Maybe the subject matter doesn't interest you. Maybe it's just too time-consuming. Or maybe it's your kid's softball season, and you don't want to miss games because the case will take a lot of time. But it's a good case, and a good fee, from a referral source you'd like to make happy by taking it.

That's when you start thinking about hiring someone. Nowadays, in large metropolitan areas, to be competitive, you may have to pay a qualified associate $15,000–$20,000 per month. While it seems like a lot, remember, now you can accept those cases and fees you would've turned down, and let your associate handle them. And the associate is still helping you move your caseload. At the same time, you're teaching them how to bring in business, which helps you. Hire the right person and teach them the right way; it works.

You grow your client base. You continually build new relationships. And you do it without sacrificing your time or your quality of life.

That's how you do it. That's how you become the rainmaker you want to be.

PATIENCE IS A VIRTUE

There's a real value in being patient, especially when cases don't come through the door every day. When I began my practice in the 1990s, after getting fired, referrals came in fairly steadily—one or two a month, like clockwork. If you plotted it on a timeline, it would look like a fairly straight, even line. For many years, things didn't fluctuate much.

But since the pandemic, it's been completely different. Now I may go two or three weeks without anything, and then all of a sudden five cases come in over the span of three days.

I don't think the shift has anything to do with crime rates or police activity. It's just how people move through life. Maybe they're too busy to call, maybe they're putting it off, hoping they don't need a lawyer, the D.A. doesn't file, or maybe they're shopping for lawyers, who knows? But the pattern has become volatile, which is why patience is so important.

If you go a couple of weeks or even a month without bringing in new business, don't panic. Don't start second-guessing everything. And don't throw away all the strong foundational work you've been doing just because it's quiet for a bit. If you're good at what you do, if you're out there making and maintaining those relationships, the cases will come. They just will. But in the meantime, there are ways to stay active and make money.

We talked earlier about making special appearances and getting on conflict lists for court-appointed cases—you can do those things if you're a little hungry, if things are slow. That's what

I did in the beginning. But I might do things differently now. Having seen the tremendous short- and long-term value of relationship networking, I would use my free time to join multiple networking groups and really hit it hard. Over time, the strategy would pay off.

Assuming you're doing it right, the referrals will always come, consistently or not. And if your base is solid enough, you can't help but be successful even if there are some slower times.

As I became more confident and the cases kept coming, I raised my hourly rate. My time became more valuable. And it's one of the most important lessons you'll learn when you go out on your own: Time really is your most precious commodity.

If your schedule is a little slow and you prefer it that way, great. Enjoy it. But if you're slow and you're itching to go faster, use the time to really stress networking. Every person you get to know is a potential referral source.

Just remember, everything takes time. As long as you're doing the right things, laying the foundation, building strong relationships, and developing your skills, success is inevitable. There are many people out there with legal problems in your area of practice. They will find you.

And if they're not? Then something's off. Maybe you're not networking correctly. Maybe you're not visible enough. But that's fixable. That's something you can work on.

The point is: be patient. Stay consistent. And keep building. The rest will come.

NO NEED TO PANIC

I really believe you should never panic because if you're doing it right, you'll always be okay, even during the slow times.

Even if things are quiet for a while, you need to have enough funds set aside for a rainy day so you can get through a month or two (or three) without stressing. As you become more successful and busier, it's smart to work with a financial planner and start putting money away. That way, when the slow periods come, and they will, you won't freak out.

For me, at this stage, if I have a slow month or two, honestly, I'm happy. It means I can catch up or even get ahead on all my cases. I can take a weekend trip to Las Vegas. I can take a day off. I actually enjoy it when it's quiet. Talk about a change in mindset over the years!

But coming up on forty years in practice, I've seen enough to know: No slow streak lasts forever. In the last five to ten years, the longest I've gone without bringing in a new case—on only one or two occasions—was just a few weeks. And then, sure enough, boom! The phone rings off the hook.

So, I don't panic. I don't need to; I've been fortunate, yes, but also, I've been intentional. I've done the right things. I've built a strong foundation. My name is out there. I've worked hard to earn a solid reputation, and I know people will find me when they need me.

Somebody's going to talk to someone I know and say, "I just got arrested," or "I need a criminal defense attorney," and my name will come up. That's why I stay calm, because I trust the systems I've put in place. People are not going to stop committing crimes, and people are not going to stop suing each other. So, it's okay for you to be patient.

Here's something interesting I've only begun reflecting on recently—something that came into sharper focus when a colleague passed away. Back when I was a younger lawyer practicing criminal defense in my county, there were about seven or eight attorneys who were at "the top." They got all the big cases. They were the ones judges called when they needed representation. They were the go-to attorneys for entertainers, politicians, athletes, you name it. Everyone knew who they were.

I remember thinking early on, *I'm as good in trial as any of them. So why am I not getting those cases*? What I've learned is that, over time, if you keep doing excellent work for your clients and building strong relationships, you slowly move up the food chain. It's not immediate. It's not flashy. But it happens. People retire. People pass away. People leave the profession. And without even realizing it, you've moved closer to the top.

Now, so deep into my career and with the base I've developed, I'm one of the names people know. In a region like mine, with maybe a couple hundred criminal defense attorneys, there are probably thirty or forty that most attorneys would recognize, and maybe five or ten who consistently handle the most significant cases. It's taken me almost four decades to get there.

But I made it because I built the right foundation and made the right decisions. I protected my reputation. I treated clients, referral sources, judges, prosecutors, and other lawyers well. And I cannot emphasize this enough: Your reputation is everything. You can never undo the damage if you harm it. You just can't.

So, when you've done all the right things over time—when you've built trust, built visibility, and maintained your integrity—you don't worry about slow weeks. You don't worry about whether another case will come through the door. Because not only will cases come in, but now they're better cases. Significant cases. And, if you want them, some of them may even come with a little bit of public attention.

That's what happens when you've put in the work and done it the right way.

KNOW YOUR VALUE

Every lawyer has credentials. So, how do you stand out? Let's say you worked at a big firm for eight years and you're now going out on your own. You bring a wealth of experience. You've worked on big cases. You've written strong briefs. You've helped secure impressive results for the firm's clients. That's real value, and it's something you should talk about in your networking.

Highlight it on your website. Include it on your CV. And don't hesitate to share it with every potential client who walks through your door. Just because you're new to running your own firm doesn't mean you're new to practicing law. You've already done the work. You've built a foundation of knowledge and credibility that clients want to know about and will benefit from.

As a rainmaker, it's your *job* to understand and communicate your value. Own it—just don't be arrogant about it.

The secret sauce, a real difference between someone who brings in the occasional case and a true rainmaker who consistently generates business, is this: the ability to relieve the client's stress and anxiety as part of earning and keeping their trust.

That's it. And there's no barrier to entry.

When you remind your clients that part of your job is to take the pressure off, that you'll answer the phone when they call, that your responses will always be as helpful and clear as possible, and your goal is to let them go about their day without overly worrying about that serious legal problem hanging over their head, you become more than just their lawyer. You become someone they respect, trust, and depend on.

And that kind of trust? It's what makes you invaluable. When someone they know needs a lawyer, they'll recommend you.

PRICED PERFECTLY

Now you know the secrets to rainmaking, but here's something important: If you set your fees too low or too high, you may find it hard to even pay your rent.

When you're figuring out how to price your services, there is a lot to consider. Let's say you just left a large firm. You know their hourly rate. You've done the same work and handled the same kinds of cases. So, you're absolutely within your rights to charge a similar rate. You're just as good, maybe better. You can also choose to charge slightly less if you think it might attract more clients, but don't undercut yourself.

Here's the mathematical approach I take. I have an hourly rate. It's my estimate of the value of an hour of my time to a client. Experience and credentials create value.

When meeting a client, if they say they want to hire me, their next question is always, "How much?" My answer is generally the same, although the numbers will differ depending on the case. Here's what I say when quoting the fee. "From what you're saying, I think I can help you. Based on my experience, I think your case will take about fifteen to twenty hours to resolve in a way you'll like." I multiply the hours by my hourly rate, knock some off if they were referred by a friend or family member, and that's the fee.

And my clients understand why the fee is what it is. I think the key is they can see, for their particular situation, why fifteen to twenty hours is probably about right. And I don't negotiate the fee. Clients sometimes try, but I don't budge. Once you start negotiating your fee, word gets around. Pretty soon, everyone will expect a discount.

This brings up something else you didn't learn in law school. You can't be afraid that a potential client will walk out and choose not to hire you. You have to be okay with that. You have to be willing to let them go. If I lose a case because I wouldn't lower my rate, that's fine. The next client will walk through the door and hire me at my full rate. And guess what? If they don't, I get my time back.

I can use the time to work on other cases, do some networking, or even play fantasy football. I'd rather miss high than take the case for too low a fee. The way I see it, the potential client needs you a lot more than you need them. You treat them respectfully, but to get the fee you deserve, you have to approach it in this manner.

You don't have to be the most expensive attorney out there, but you deserve to charge your worth. Why? Because in addition to doing great legal work, you offer something many lawyers don't: accessibility and empathy. With most attorneys, especially at large firms, clients have to go through multiple gatekeepers just to get someone on the phone. Yours do not.

My clients get my cell phone number. And I only have one cell phone. If they call on a Saturday, I pick up. Direct access is invaluable to clients and potential clients. It is a key to reducing their stress and anxiety. And you can be sure referral sources very much appreciate you being available to someone they entrusted to you.

Whenever I tell a new client they get that kind of access, it always leaves a mark, in a good way. And let's take it one step further. Let's say someone calls about a new matter at 12:00 p.m. on a Tuesday. That call needs to be returned by 12:30 p.m. the same day. Because if you don't quickly call them back, they might look elsewhere.

Responsiveness makes a strong impression. I can't tell you how many times people have said to me, "Thank you for calling me back so quickly, just hearing back from you makes me feel better about my situation."

The truth is, at the end of the day, you may not be so different from those other attorneys the client might talk to. But the client hires *you* because they know they can actually reach you, and you've demonstrated to them that you care about the outcome of their matter.

I've seen it happen over and over again.

A word of caution, though. You never want to be hired by people who are simply looking for the lowest fee. They're not going to be good clients. What *you* offer clients, most lawyers do not. So, get what you're worth.

THOSE PRICE SHOPPERS

At the end of the day, if someone is only concerned about price, they're probably not going to appreciate the value you bring to the table, especially when it comes to reducing their stress and anxiety. If their sole focus is money, then yeah, you might cost more than someone else, and they may not hire you. That's okay.

You treat clients well, you explain what the legal process looks like, and they know they can always reach you. You earn what you collect. But if a potential client is just shopping around for the cheapest lawyer? I don't even want to talk to them.

Because their criteria isn't: "Who's the best lawyer I can afford?" It's "Who's the cheapest lawyer I can find?" And I'm not trying to be the cheapest lawyer; in fact, the experience I give them is the opposite—they are well cared for.

The discount lawyer doesn't have time to return phone calls. They can't. They're too busy chasing volume so they can keep the lights on. They have to take in a lot of cases because their fees are too low. That's not the kind of business I want to run.

I like to have just enough cases, so I'm able to deliver what the client really needs—helping them get through the worst time of their life. That matters. That's the value.

KEEPING EXPENSES LOW

As a law firm owner, it's imperative that you keep your expenses low, especially at the start. You don't want to be paying out too much before your income is steady.

At your old firm, you may have had a legal assistant who did everything for you. For example, new lawyers often summarize depositions. Early in your career, you may have too. Five or six years in, you had someone to do it for you. But when you go out on your own, you may not have anyone. You may need to do the more menial work again. You might have to run down to the courthouse to file something or pick up a document because you no longer have a staff member or don't want to spend the money on a messenger. All of these factor into your bottom line.

Office expenses can be kept down with a smaller space, a more modest location, or by sharing space with other attorneys. You can split costs like the copier, scanner, and kitchen supplies.

Another way to save money is to rethink your staffing. Do you need a full-time receptionist, or could an answering service handle it? You'll also want to think about whether you need a paralegal when you start the new firm, or if you want to wait a while.

Here's another place where you can save money: All those "Top Ten Lawyer" plaques you'll get pitched as soon as you go out on your own. They'll say, "Pay $300 and hang this award on your wall." Don't. It's just marketing fluff. And worse, they'll keep charging your credit card year after year until you cancel. You don't need it.

And finally, don't overlook your personal expenses. In the early years, you want to keep as much money in the firm as possible. That's how you build your six-month safety net. Buy instead of rent if you can, but don't overspend on a home. Put off the world tour or luxury car. For the first two or three years, be lean.

The more pressure you put on yourself financially, the more cases you'll have to take, and not always the ones you want. The nicer the car, the bigger the house, the more stress and anxiety you bring on yourself.

But if you can run a lean office and personal life for three to five years, until you really get your practice going, that's ideal. Keep your overhead low, and you'll sleep better at night.

Now that you know how to build your practice, let's talk about how to drive business to you. We'll start with networking in the next chapter.

CHAPTER 5

NETWORKING: THE ENGINE OF GROWTH

As a criminal defense attorney, I like to think I shine during closing arguments. It's like being an actor up on stage, with twelve jurors, a judge, and a courtroom audience all focused on me. But believe it or not, I'm actually an introvert.

I have no trouble standing up in front of a jury and telling them why my client is not guilty of the crime. I can do it in my sleep. I don't get nervous. It's what I do. And in the moment, I kind of feel like, hey, everyone's got to look at me. It's like a play, and I'm the star. They have to listen because there's no one else speaking.

But going to a networking meeting? Totally different. You might only know the one person there, who invited you. Suddenly, you have to introduce yourself to people you've never met, shake hands, give them a short pitch about who you are, what you do, and how you could bring them value. You also have to remember to first ask them about what they do. You start thinking, *How do I talk about referrals? Should there be a financial incentive for them to refer clients to me? How do we build a referral relationship?*

This skill set, which you need to develop to become a rainmaker, is completely different than being in a courtroom. But it matters just as much.

For the first thirty years of my career, I felt like I didn't need to market myself. I was comfortable and busy with a steady stream of cases.

But nearly a decade ago, everything started to shift.

In one case, my opposing counsel was a really good guy. I could see that he and I were very similar in how we went all-out for our clients. One day, he said to me, "Hey, I'm a member of a particular marketing group. Want to go to a networking event with me? I'd like to bring a guest, and you'd enjoy it." I didn't have anything scheduled for lunch the next day, so I said yes.

That networking meeting changed everything.

The importance of networking had never *really* occurred to me before that. After all, people who refer to you will always refer to you, right? No. They won't. They may have less opportunity, start referring to someone else, move, retire, or worse. You simply cannot take referral sources for granted.

What I heard at the networking meeting made so much sense that I signed up on the spot, not for one, but for two years. It was the beginning of my foray into marketing my law firm. I saw immediately how powerful it could be for my business, and kind of kicked myself for not realizing it much earlier in my career. And I was right. I've made an incredible amount of money through the relationships I've formed there. I never would have made that kind of money if I hadn't gone to lunch with opposing counsel. One person. One meeting. Amazing, right?

The real relationships happen in your networking groups.

There is no shortage of ways to market your firm, like joining a bar association, but as I've mentioned, those tend to be less effective when it comes to actually bringing in business. For example, let's say you join your county's Bar Association. Maybe you even run for president or vice president of the group, thinking the visibility will help build your referral base. It might, to a point. You'll definitely meet attorneys. But chances are, a lot of them do the same kind of work you do, so they're not likely to refer cases your way. That's not to say joining a bar association is a bad idea. It's just not as powerful as being active in a true networking group where people are looking to build referral relationships across professions.

But networking is where the best referrals come from.

NETWORKING AND MARKETING

I actually grew my client base at a nice pace before I joined the networking group. I was doing pretty well without the group. What networking did was put things over the top. It added another piece to everything else I was already doing. It allowed me to create some long-term relationships I really value, both professionally and personally. And like any business owner who thinks about where the next case is coming from, the group has created so many additional referral sources that I no longer stress about the next case.

What a good networking and marketing plan does, if effectively carried out, is give you a kind of assurance. Not a guarantee, but a strong foundation. If other parts of your plan do not work out, you'll have sufficient work to make a living and figure out what else to do.

So, think of networking and marketing as a base. Here's something to take away: Consider networking to be part of your job. It requires as much attention as does any case. It deserves a certain number of hours of attention every week, just like your cases. It gives you confidence that you'll earn enough to hit your long-term goals. Because if you do networking and marketing right, it won't fail. It literally cannot fail.

MARKETING ISN'T ABOUT BEING FOUND—IT'S ABOUT BEING REFERRED

I'll be the first to tell you that having a website is important. But here's the thing: My website isn't designed to attract new clients from Google. It's not about search engine optimization (SEO), and personally, I think for my firm, SEO is a waste of money.

As a sole practitioner, you're never going to be able to spend enough to stay ahead of someone else on a Google results page. Maybe you'll show up ahead of them once out of every ten clicks, but even then, the cases you get aren't going to be your ideal clients. People clicking around for "Southern California criminal defense attorney" are not the types who are really invested in society and have a lot to lose with a criminal conviction. They are not the types of people I'm looking to work with. It's just not worth it. You'll get much better traction by building a strong network and generating word-of-mouth.

There is no better way to earn people's trust than by getting to know them. That's how the best referrals happen.

I don't do SEO. My website isn't built for cold leads or casual internet searches. It's designed for other lawyers, especially newer lawyers who don't have a go-to criminal defense guy. They can look me up, see what I do, get a feel for how I work, and understand why my credentials will help them look good, so they will feel confident sending clients. And if a client sees it, great.

Back in the '90s, I advertised on a local all-sports radio station and had a now-famous host record my ad. I got maybe one or two DUI cases over a year, and they were people who were searching for the lowest-priced attorney. Looking back, it confirms that word-of-mouth referrals are far more valuable than any cold lead from a search engine or radio spot.

Now, my website has some short videos—nothing fancy. Just a couple of minutes each. But they're there so other attorneys can get a sense of who I am and how I work. If their clients ask them questions, they can even watch a quick video and feel a little more prepared before recommending me.

So yes, my website works, and it works well, but not in the traditional SEO sense. It's built to speak to other lawyers. It's there to build trust and relationships, not to chase clicks. And that's exactly how I want it.

If you're just starting out and looking to build your practice, I'd say this: Set a goal in the first year to find four or five lawyers who will refer to you. That's essentially what I did after I was fired. I focused on building those relationships. The next year, I found more. Then even more. Eventually, I joined a networking group, and it really took off.

Now, I have ninety or so people who regularly refer clients. Perfect. That's all I need. And my website supports my marketing strategy, not by pulling in strangers, but by reinforcing the trust of the people who already know me, some who just met me, and those who are about to get to know me.

Let me give you one more example.

As I was working on this chapter, I got a call about a serious financial crime case. The client was in jail, facing twenty years. Non-citizen. Deportation on the table. Family. Kids. Serious stuff.

But someone else was calling around on his behalf, and after describing how bad the client's situation was, they told me, "We're looking for the least expensive lawyer we can find."

I said, "Okay, that's fine, but why?"

They said, "He has plenty of money. He just doesn't think lawyers are worth it."

That's when I knew I wasn't the right lawyer for them. I told them I appreciated the call, but I wasn't the guy they were looking for.

As soon as I hear someone is looking for the cheapest lawyer, I know it's not going to be a good fit. I'm never going to compete on price because people who shop for the cheapest lawyer almost always turn out to be the worst clients. They tend to take more of my time and don't follow my advice. You want good clients, not difficult people clogging your busy day.

In my view, that's the difference between SEO leads and real referrals. One is a numbers game. The other is about trust.

Give me trust every time.

CHOOSE RELATIONSHIPS OVER HEADLINES

I've represented entertainers and athletes. In my opinion, it doesn't make a difference to your bottom line if you handle high-profile cases that show up on national or local news. I don't think you get more clients just because people see you on television standing next to someone famous. It might be someone else's thing, but it's never been mine. I know lawyers who live for the media spotlight.

If you want to take on a high-profile case because it's kind of fun or you like the buzz that comes with it, fine. Just understand it comes with baggage.

In my experience, media members literally walk from courtroom to courtroom to see if anything interesting is going on. If so, they might report on it. And most media members are great—they're hard working, they report accurately, and they're doing their job of keeping the public informed. However, early in my career, I had a bad experience with one member of the media.

I had my first high-profile case. We got a great result at trial, where we were able to literally prove a key prosecution witness lied on the stand, and the jury came back with a quick not guilty verdict. After the case was over, I spoke with a reporter who had covered it.

And then when the story came out, the reporter misquoted me. It wasn't even close, and I thought it made the prosecutor look bad. I told an attorney friend I respected about it, and he just said, "Why'd you talk to the press at all?" And you know what? I had no good answer. Maybe it was ego. I don't know. But he was right: "Lesson learned. It never comes out the way you want." He nailed it.

Fast forward to about two decades later, and I had a big murder case with the media everywhere. When the case ended, I walked out of the courtroom with my co-counsel, and it was a mob scene. Microphones, cameras, the whole thing. We turned to the bailiff and said, "Can you get us out the back door?" I didn't want to talk to anyone. We'd just gotten a great result, but I had no interest in being on the evening news. I figured if they mention my name, great. But there's nothing in it for me. It won't come out right. And I don't have a face for television anyway.

Honestly, I don't think representing high-profile clients has made a bit of difference in my practice. What has made the difference is that I return phone calls. I treat people well. I care about their cases. We develop a relationship.

The famous ones? They don't add anything extra. Not to me. That's also why I'd never put my name on a bus bench or billboard. The people who are going to call you from those ads aren't the kind of clients you want to work with.

I'd rather be boutique. I'd rather take time to network, get to know a lot of referral sources, and when they send someone, meet with the client, connect with them, and really understand their situation. That's where the best fees come from. That's where the best long-term relationships come from. That's how you avoid problems later, like a client filing a bar complaint when things don't go exactly as they hoped. It's all about the relationship.

Now, when times are slow, or you're a little nervous about making the mortgage, you might be tempted to take a case you wouldn't normally take. Be cautious. You might think, *Okay, I can handle this one*, even if your gut says otherwise. And sometimes it works out. But other times, the case turns out to be way more trouble than it's worth. It drains your time, your energy, and you look back and think, *Why did I take that one*? But in the moment, it felt like the right call.

That's all part of building a practice. You learn as you go. You figure out what works and what doesn't. And for me? Chasing media attention never worked. Handling cases outside my expertise never worked.

Relationships did. Always have. Always will.

CHAPTER 6

HUSTLE, SHOW UP, REPEAT

When I found myself out of a job with only $4,000 in the bank, I had absolutely no experience running my own law firm and zero idea about what I was doing. I'd always worked for other people. I'd never been on my own.

So, I told myself I was going to do two things. *First*, I was going to be in court. *A lot*. Why? Because that's where people see you. Other lawyers, judges, and even people sitting in the gallery. They see how you show up. They see what kind of job you do.

And when they're impressed? They start thinking about you for referrals.

Believe it or not, judges, and even retired judges, refer cases to attorneys they trust will do a good job. Prosecutors also refer cases to lawyers they've dealt with in the courtroom. Over the years, I've gotten some good cases from judges and prosecutors. Sounds crazy, but it's true.

Second, I was going to take just about any criminal case I could. In those early years, I couldn't afford to be selective, so I took every case I could. Maybe I didn't love the type of case. Maybe I had to lower my fee just to get it. But it got me into court. It built my presence. It allowed me to do a good job for the client, in front of prosecutors and judges, who could refer me to others if the opportunity arose. And it built momentum. I kept my eye on the ball.

Even then, when I was just getting started, I treated every client like gold. If I got them a good result and treated them well, they would turn around and start referring people to me. That's how it grew for me, and that's how it will grow for you.

LEARNING BY DOING

We talked earlier about joining conflict panels in order to receive court-appointed work when you're new to your practice.

The pay is low, but the value? Incredible.

I completed a lot of jury trials to verdict while I was accepting court appointments. Trial after trial. Preliminary hearing after preliminary hearing. These were tough cases, gang cases, murder cases, juvenile cases, third-strike cases, and complicated theft cases—hard cases to settle. Some of my clients were as difficult and notorious as they come.

But that's how I learned to be a lawyer. I had to build relationships with clients who didn't hire me; basically, I was assigned to them. And I had to figure out how to make it work. It also put me in front of every judge and prosecutor in my county who handled criminal cases. They saw me. They observed how I worked. That's how I built my reputation.

Between being appointed on cases by the court and covering special appearances for other lawyers, in the five years after I began my own practice, I literally never turned anything down.

What did that give me?

- More visibility in court
- More connections with lawyers and judges
- Experience dealing with other people's clients
- A little money to pay the bills

And I learned that you've got to be careful when you're standing in for another lawyer. I had to represent them well, too—not just the client. So, the work helped build my reputation with other attorneys.

BUILDING A PRACTICE, ONE SLICE AT A TIME

If you picture my early business like a pizza, the slices were:

- Conflict panel appointments
- A few cases I brought in myself
- Special appearances and work for other lawyers

That's what paid the bills for a while.

When I was just starting out, I asked to be on every panel out there, including the list where I represented minors.

Juvenile Court was great. I liked working with kids. The cases moved fast. I had to deal with the minors, their parents, judges, prosecutors, and probation officers. It taught me a lot—not just about law, but about communication.

To get on those panels, I had to do the legwork. I tracked down different court administrators and judges. I told them about my background. I agreed to their rates. I filled out applications. I was patient as most panels opened up only once a year. Back then, a felony case in my county might pay $450. Seriously.

But it's what I needed to do to build the kind of practice I wanted.

I made sure I was always available. If a judge's clerk called with a court appointment, I arrived in the courtroom within thirty minutes to an hour to accept the case and meet the client. If I couldn't make it, I'd let them know when I'd be there, then I'd arrive on time. And I *always* thanked the judge and clerk. I figured there were twenty-five or thirty lawyers on the list. Being appreciative couldn't hurt.

Finally, I was bringing in enough of my own cases, so taking a $450 felony case didn't make financial sense. But accepting those cases at such low rates got me where I needed to be. I knew the judges. I knew the prosecutors. They trusted me despite my being a strong advocate for my clients. I knew what I was doing. I knew how to treat clients. That's how I learned.

And handling cases that are not your own is not just for criminal defense attorneys. No matter your area of practice, you can do the same thing. Reach out to lawyers at bigger firms. Offer to take overflow work. If they don't want to do discovery, a deposition, or a trial, offer to do it. Be respectful, be on time, be available, and be the person the lawyer can count on. Hustle!

Let's say a family law lawyer only takes cases in her county. Driving farther away doesn't fit her practice. You say, "Give me your out-of-county cases. I'll do a great job, and you keep a good piece of the fee." The client's family now thinks the lawyer's firm handles cases anywhere, and she gets the credit. You get experience and make some money. Everyone wins.

If you are not a litigator, this process still works. It just depends on the type of practice you're in. Take transactional lawyers, for example. They can be overwhelmed with work, too. Maybe someone does homeowners' association work. Let's say they already have four or five big HOAs as clients, and now a new one wants to come on board, but the lawyer's just too busy. Well, guess what? If they have someone they trust who can handle the transactional piece and do a good job, they can still onboard the new client, have you work with them, and take a piece of it. These strategies work just as well for transactional lawyers as they do for litigators.

The first three to five years of building your practice might look different for each type of lawyer. But the principle is the same. There are lawyers out there who are way too busy and would love to hand off work, especially if they trust you and you're willing to give them a piece in return. You just have to meet them, then build the relationship.

But I am not going to sugarcoat it: Building a practice from scratch for long-term profitability is hard. But if you're willing to hustle, work for a little less, be helpful, take less glamorous work, and treat people well, it can be done. That's how I did it. And I wouldn't change a thing.

RED FLAG CLIENTS

One of the things lawyers always think about is the risk; if a case doesn't go the client's way, they might get sued for malpractice.

I've been really lucky in that regard. But I have friends who haven't. And it's not just about getting sued. There are plenty of other things clients can do to create problems. They can fire you mid-case. In criminal cases, where you're typically paid a flat fee, you now owe them a refund for any unused portion. So now you're doing accounting, trying to figure out what work you've done, and it takes up your time. It pulls energy away from your practice and away from your family. It's a drain. You don't need it.

That's why your intake interview is so important. That's where the relationship starts. It's not just about whether they're hiring you. It's about whether you're hiring them. Because let's be honest: Taking a case is like getting married. You're going to be tied to this person for a while, and you don't want the relationship to end badly.

So, when you meet with a potential client, you've got to really evaluate them and not just think about the fee. Make judgments about their personality. Be selfish and always protect yourself.

As much as they want you to, you can't promise a client a particular outcome. It's unethical. You can't say, "I guarantee the judge will do this." If you've been around a long time like I have, you might have a pretty good idea, but you never really know. You'd rather the client be happily surprised with the result, rather than angry because you didn't get them the promised result.

And even if someone looks great on paper, they've got a good job, no criminal history, you still have to ask, "Is this person going to be a good client?" Because you could get blindsided. Maybe you feel good about the case and think, *They're probably not going to go to jail.* And then you find out later they didn't tell you about a prior robbery conviction. Now they're looking at serious jail time. They'll say, "Oh, I told you." No, they didn't. Now they're lying to you, and soon they'll be second-guessing everything, including you.

That's why the first interview is so important. You've got to pay attention to how and what they say, whether they make excuses or blame others, whether they're accountable, and whether they answered your direct questions. Red flags come up fast.

For example, when someone talks a lot about money, it's a red flag. Now, obviously, in criminal defense, where you're paid up front, money's going to be part of the conversation. That's normal. But sometimes they're hyper-focused on it, "How much is this going to cost?" "Are you going to charge me if you file motions?" "What if we go to court a few extra times?" Those are red flags. It tells me they're already looking for ways to challenge the fee, and it usually means trouble. I'm going to pass on the case.

Another red flag: someone who says, "Can you hurry and get my case done?" Especially in criminal cases, it's almost never realistic. You might want to get them into an anger management program, which could take twelve weeks. Or a rehab program that lasts six months, sometimes longer.

Why this strategy? Because the court wants to see progress over time before extending the great offer you're hoping to get the client. If you rush, you'll miss the opportunity to show how well the client can do without the need for a jail sentence, and the results suffer. So, if someone's pushing to fast-track their case, it's not a good sign.

Now the flip side. Good clients are the ones invested in life. They've got something to lose: a job, a professional license, a family, their reputation. They care about avoiding jail. They care about charges being dismissed. Those clients are much more likely to listen, to follow your advice, and to trust your experience. They just want to get through it the right way, with minimum consequences. Those are, by far, the easiest clients to represent.

DON'T BE THE DISCOUNT LAWYER

I really believe this: The only way you're going to survive charging very low fees is by taking on way too many cases. It's the only way to make the numbers work. But when you're dealing with too much volume, there's no way you can spend meaningful time on any one case. And if you don't have the time, the outcome won't be as good. It just won't.

And in your haste to work on each case in your inflated caseload, you run the risk of making a critical mistake, which will get you sued. At a minimum, you've done a disservice to your client. It's a rabbit hole that's hard to escape. What do you think the lawyer who referred the case will think when the client badmouths you to them?

That's a really important distinction for any lawyer who's just starting out. You have to resist the temptation to be the most inexpensive lawyer. You have to stick to your guns. Know your worth.

When you're broke and starting from zero, hustle is the strategy. Take the cases others don't want, show up everywhere, and treat every client like they matter. Every appearance builds skill, trust, and a name that not only your clients will remember, but judges, prosecutors, and other lawyers will respect. That leads to referrals and future business.

Let's talk more about those referrals in the next chapter.

CHAPTER 7

THE POWER OF REFERRALS AND RELATIONSHIPS

Part of your decision-making process in how you allocate your marketing dollars involves the question of whether you'd rather get a referral through word-of-mouth or by some other means, right? And word-of-mouth is just such a superior form of referral compared to anything else.

Word-of-mouth is better because the person making the recommendation is showing the referral they're invested in you. That they trust you. That they trust you enough to tell the referral, "You should call Bob, he'll get you the best possible result, and you'll like working with him too." And that trust means a great deal to the potential client. That trust carries a lot more weight than just about anything else during your first meeting, when they're still deciding whether to hire you, at the fee you quoted. But you go into the meeting literally with a head start.

> **A bus bench, a park bench, the back of a bus, a random television commercial, or a radio ad; none compare to a reputable person telling a client to call you because you're the best at what you do, and you're great to work with as well. Master this, and you can be a rainmaker.**

Then, when the case is over, and the client knows you've done everything you can to help them reduce their stress and anxiety, the relationship really cements itself. They've seen the work. They've seen all the discovery, the police reports, the witness statements, and the lab results. They've seen the motions you filed. They've seen you in court. They've seen how you interact with the prosecutor and the judge. They've seen how hard you work. They've seen how you were able to get them a good result. They trust you'll promptly return their calls and be patient with their questions and suggestions.

Who do you think they'll turn to if they, or anyone they know, needs help? Not the inexpensive lawyer—that's for sure. And when they tell the person who recommended you, even better!

Most people, after going through all the emotional turmoil of a court case, want to maintain a relationship with you. Because you're a good person to know. You've shown up for them. I get a lot of referrals from prior clients for exactly that reason: Because we had a solid relationship. They trusted me, and I earned their trust.

A CHANCE ENCOUNTER

I was sitting in a courtroom many years ago, and there was a very nice attorney who spoke very little English. It was definitely not his first language.

The judge was difficult for the attorney to understand. The judge was polite and respectful, not yelling, but she was using a lot of legal terminology with the lawyer, and both were clearly frustrated. Try as he might, the attorney simply did not understand the judge due to the language barrier. He had filed something incorrectly, and the judge was explaining it, but it was obvious the lawyer was struggling.

Even though he was a lawyer, it was obvious he wasn't a criminal defense attorney. But he was handling a criminal case. I knew the judge well, so during a pause in their back-and-forth, I quietly asked the attorney if I could assist him, and he agreed. I then asked, "Judge, may I speak with him for a moment?" She said yes and agreed to call the case again in a few minutes.

So, we went outside, and I said, "This is what you need to tell the judge, 'x, y, z,' and you'll be good." He was very appreciative.

The case was a big deal. The client had stolen a lot of money from an overseas company, and although the client was arrested in Orange County, the case was also tied to another state, and it would be sent there. That's why the judge was being so particular. Extradition, conflict of laws, International stuff, big money. The lawyer was out of his depth.

The attorney went back into the courtroom, the case was called again, and he said the right words, and the hearing wrapped up. Afterward, he asked if we could talk in the courthouse cafeteria. I said, "Sure." He told me, "I want you to handle this case." And I said, "Well, I'm happy to help, but it's your case, it's your fee." And he literally said, "She's my client, I care about her and the family. I want her to have an experienced lawyer, and you're clearly the best person for her. Quote her whatever you think is fair."

And at that point in my career, given the seriousness of the case, the location where it would be moved, and the stakes, I knew it would be the biggest fee I had ever quoted.

Then the lawyer said, "You don't need to pay me a referral fee. I really appreciate how you helped, because I was about to faint." I remember saying, "You don't need to do that," and he laughed. But he meant it. He referred the case to me.

I took the case. It became one of the first cases where I had to travel extensively out of state. It wasn't federal, it was in state court, which meant I had to get local counsel. The referring attorney, local counsel, and I all became friends and started referring cases back and forth.

I flew there seven or eight times for the case. And it was a good experience. We had a nice D.A. and a great judge. One day, the judge took us into chambers and said, "Mr. Hartmann, what are you doing *here*?" And I said, "Your Honor, I've always wanted to visit here and handle a case in this building, so it's a win-win."

The judge laughed and said, "You're not a Dodgers fan, are you? I hate the Dodgers."

The D.A. was laughing too, and he said, "I'm planning a trip for my family to Disneyland next summer. Maybe you could recommend a hotel?" This was all in front of the judge, and I said, "Absolutely, my office is pretty close." Nothing improper, but it shows how the simple act of being nice to people can really help a client. It's not an illusion.

The case, where the client was potentially looking at many years in prison, was resolved with what we'd call "credit for time served." She was in jail when I met her, and by the time we were done, she was free. It was a really good result. The in-chambers conference is not the reason, but honestly, I believe the relaxed, informal nature of our conversation nurtured trust between me, the judge, and D.A. So, when I made certain representations regarding the client and the mitigation, I thought it would be a little easier for them to believe my comments.

The attorney who referred the case was just astonished when I called with the good news. He told me, "Be prepared to get a letter from the client's family." Sure enough, I got an email inviting me to meet them in their country. The client's parents said they wanted to fly me out, just to take me to dinner to thank me for what I'd done for their daughter.

I remember thinking, *You don't need to pay for the trip; I'll just meet you over there.* So, I planned a trip, since I had never been to that part of the world. The fee I had received was enough to justify the trip, where I could create a potential new referral source in the parents, who had lots of professional connections and potential referral sources in the United States.

What I remember most is dinner. The parents didn't speak the best English, but we were able to communicate. And I remember they said I had "saved their family." In their culture, family is everything. They told me they didn't even know how to express their appreciation. The original attorney had told them their daughter was looking at seven to ten years in prison. And here she was, home and at dinner with her parents and me. On another continent!

They said, "We don't know how you did it." And I joked, "It was easy. I just talked about baseball." They looked at me like I had two heads.

Then they commented, "Oh, so the American system is like our country. It's all about who you know." And I remember saying, "Well, it's not like that. If you treat people in the court respectfully, create trust, and advocate for a client, it's amazing what can happen."

So, not only did I get the case and the fee. I met some incredible overseas referral sources. And the same attorney has probably referred four cases in twenty-five years, and they're among the biggest cases I've ever had. The family I met for dinner? Two great referrals over the years.

And it all started because I simply asked the judge, "Your Honor, can we take a few minutes? Can I talk to the attorney?"

NURTURING A RELATIONSHIP

I normally try to refer cases back to the attorney who referred to me, if I can. But if I can't, they're usually very happy just getting a referral fee, a small portion of the fee paid by the client.

If the person referring isn't an attorney, it's a little different. You need to touch base with them every ninety days—always be "top of mind." That could be a "How's everything going?" email, or an invite to grab a drink. Maybe you heard they wrote a blog, and you give them a great comment. Whatever it is, stay in contact, and find some commonality so there's a reason to keep the conversation going.

For example, I know a retired schoolteacher who lives about seventy-five miles away. She's not a lawyer. You'd think I wouldn't have a lot in common with her, but she's one of those people who magically, mysteriously sends a lot of business.

So how do I nurture the relationship? Every year, my charitable foundation puts on a wine event. And every year, I get two tickets for her and her husband. They aren't free. They cost me about $800. But she gets those tickets as a thank-you, and I spend time with them at the event.

I also have a friend who's a real estate agent. Over the years, she's referred a few really good cases. When she needed legal advice, I was able to recommend someone who really helped her. And, on two occasions, she's referred friends who became legal assistants. She's always out there for me. She gets two tickets as well, and we always share a laugh over a glass of wine.

There are other people in my network who get tickets too. My firm spends several thousand dollars on wine event tickets every year. I'll invite ten to twenty people, usually among my best referral sources, who like wine, and they can bring a guest and enjoy a beautiful Sunday afternoon tasting wine near the beach.

Everyone eats, drinks, and mingles. And for my group, I host an after-party, where we all go out for pizza. I take the whole group because after a day of food and wine, what we really need is more food, right? But really, it's just about sitting around a table together. It gives people a chance to connect with each other. And, I'm the common link. But now they're meeting each other: a realtor, a retired teacher, a lawyer, whoever. That's where the return on investment comes in. It's a small investment to thank people who have helped me so much. It's a fun day for everyone, and it's really about showing appreciation.

In addition to holiday cards, for some referral sources, especially if I know what kind of wine they like, I'll send them a special bottle. I've built a lot of relationships with winemakers over the years, so I'll get them a beautiful, hand-carved wooden box with two or three bottles of great wine. The box includes a note thanking them for their trust and referrals.

For other referral sources, I'll send out gift certificates. Maybe there's a hot new restaurant in town. I'll get them a gift certificate so they can enjoy a nice evening out.

The gifts I send are not tied to a specific case. It's just a thank-you for their trust, and a way to express my appreciation, while at the same time continuing the relationship.

The fun part is when they send back a nice text or email. I've had people say, "I'm serving the wine at Christmas dinner," or "This made my day." It's just a small gesture, but it goes a long way toward ensuring the relationship you have put a lot of effort into is nurtured and continues.

At the end of the day, rainmaking is really about relationships. What matters more than wine, gifts, or food is how I treat people a referral source sends over for legal help. Because I guarantee you, the first thing the referral does after meeting me is call the referral source and say either, "Bob was a total knucklehead," or "We really liked him."

Nurture referrals like gold. Call people back right away. Give them the red-carpet treatment. Do a great job, follow up, and be the one they can count on.

That's step one. Step two is to thank the person who sent you the referral. And honestly, that approach has been enormously successful for me.

REFERRAL FEES

You'll need to decide early on, as part of your marketing strategy, whether you will pay referral fees to attorneys who refer business to you. Many lawyers will only refer cases to attorneys who pay referral fees; others do not care. So, whether to pay referral fees and even accept them yourself, it's important to carefully think through the ethical guidelines when you start.

You must understand the rules regarding referral fees in your state—a violation of those rules at a minimum is an ethics violation, and in some situations, a crime.

In California, the amount of the referral fee and the identity of the attorney receiving it must be disclosed to the client. And the resulting total fee paid by the client cannot be "unconscionable." It has to be reasonable and cannot exceed what would normally be charged without the referral fee. Also, lawyers may not pay referral fees to non-attorneys.

Some attorneys don't believe in accepting referral fees. Others, like me, believe they're part of doing business and are necessary. That's just the reality. So, it's important that lawyers, new to their own practice, ask potential referral sources about referral fees. Now, you may want to be subtle when you bring it up, or simply be direct. But one way or another, you need to know where the other attorney stands.

I tend to be pretty direct. I'll ask people whether they require a referral fee. Is it an easy conversation to have? No. Is it necessary? Yes. Because a lot of lawyers want a referral fee, and they won't refer cases to you unless they're going to get one. So, you need to know.

Here's an example: Let's say you have a friend who practices personal injury, and you refer to them. Then you meet another personal injury lawyer who you think could be a good referral source. Normally, another personal injury lawyer may not refer to you, given that you are not able to refer back. Paying referral fees allows you to have more than one personal injury lawyer referral source. Even though you're not sending them cases, you are doing something to help their bottom line—and you have to have this conversation with them up front.

Some attorneys don't expect a fee at all. They'll send you a case, and forget about it, and when they get a check in the mail, they're shocked. You'll get an email saying, "Oh wow, thank you. I wasn't expecting this. This is a day at Disneyland for the family. Thank you so much." That kind of thing? It really cultivates the relationship.

I have a friend from college, an enormously successful lawyer, who refers one or two cases a year. And every time, he says, "Bob, I don't believe in referral fees. Don't pay me anything." So, what do you think I do? Once a year, he gets a gift certificate. I know his favorite restaurant. He gets a gift card so he and his wife can have a great night out together.

I literally don't care if he says not to pay him a referral fee; I still send him *something* at Christmas. I make a lot of money thanks to him. But it's not about the money, it's about showing appreciation. My friend and his wife get to enjoy a nice evening, and he knows I'm grateful. A gesture like that isn't necessary, but it keeps the connection fresh and alive. And more importantly, he knows when he sends a person to me, especially if it is a client who's important to him, I'm going to handle it professionally. They'll get a good result and be treated well. And my relationship with his client will reflect well on him.

As a lawyer who strives to help the client as much as possible, a good result makes me feel great. As a rainmaker, what really matters is that the client is happy and my referral source looks great. I believe it's never just about referral fees. It's all about relationships. Because I put so much effort into the client and their experience, they're going to try hard to refer, whether or not I pay a referral fee. What matters most is how well you take care of the client. There's nothing more important.

Here's how I try to handle any referral. The moment the call comes in, I know what to do. If I can, I'll talk with them right then. If necessary, I'll return their phone call, literally, as soon as possible. Because the quicker you speak with the potential client, the better they're going to feel. The less they're going to panic. The less they're going to worry about their professional license, their job, or their reputation. The more they'll appreciate me and the referral source. And, the more likely it is that they'll hire me.

I would dread a text from a referral source saying, "My referral is waiting for you to call her back."

So even if I'm in court, I'll contact the new client right away. Let's say I get a text from my friend: "Hey, I'm sending you so-and-so." And then the call comes in while I'm sitting in the courtroom.

You know what I'll do? Ask the clerk if my case can be called in fifteen minutes. Then I step out into the hallway and call the client. "Hey, I'm in court right now, but I got your message. I'm going to call you back at 5 p.m. I've set aside an hour just for you. We'll have plenty of time to talk, and I'll be in front of my computer so I can take notes and learn more about you."

Do you know how good that makes someone feel?

Do you know how good that makes the referring person look?

These are the kinds of things that aren't about referral fees. They're not about gifts. But they add incredible value to the referral source.

Now, if you're just starting out, I get it. Sending someone a referral fee can feel scary. You're thinking, *I don't even have money coming in yet!* But you know what? Trust that you're making a good business decision. You might never have gotten the case without the referral fee, and you're making money at the end of the day. Take good care of the client, and the attorney will send you more business. And who knows, one day the attorney may send you a really big case that makes you really glad you began the referral relationship.

STAYING IN TOUCH

For attorneys running their own practice, it's critical to develop and maintain a spreadsheet containing the contact information for your referral sources. I don't mean just a bunch of names. I mean addresses, emails, cell phones, everything you need to easily reach them and track who they send to you. It allows you to easily create holiday card lists, move referral sources on and off the list, track how often you reach out to them, and keep track of when you need to contact them again.

Stay in periodic contact with your referral sources, because your practice cannot exist without them. You know the expression "out of sight, out of mind." It's really true when it comes to people who refer business to you. An attorney may lose your contact information or literally forget about you if they only have a referral opportunity once every couple of years.

One way to stay in touch and top-of-mind is to send holiday cards. Put it on your calendar for November 1st. You'll want to pick out a card, have them printed with your firm name, email address, and cell phone—and send them out. It's a small thing, but it keeps you top-of-mind, and it's part of your professional image. Send a card to anyone who might refer business.

Want to stand out even more to potential referral sources, clients, and friends who already send you work? Send out a Thanksgiving card with a theme of gratitude. Don't wait until two weeks before Christmas.

A great project for your legal assistant is to task them with the holiday card assignment, and to give you a reminder about who you need to check in on. Make it your goal that once you get a name on that list, they never leave it.

CLIENT CARE

It's really important to remember that generating referrals is not about sending wine or gifts. It's about taking great care of the client who was referred to you. That's the whole thing. If someone sends you a client and you drop the ball or don't treat the client well, you're not getting another one. Period.

The opposite is also true. When someone refers a case to you, after the intake meeting, the client is going to walk out and call the referral source from the car and tell them what they think of you. Imagine the referring attorney receiving that call, and the client says they had a tremendous experience with you! And when you do a great job, both in caring for the client and getting them a good result, the single referral can turn into five more. It grows from there.

Of course, client care starts with that initial meeting, and includes doing a great job for them in court while, at the same time, reducing their stress and anxiety by being empathic.

One big part of client care is being competent to handle their case. It seems self-evident, but we've all seen attorneys handling cases they shouldn't have taken.

Let's say you're handling transactional matters, and someone calls you about a criminal matter. The worst thing you can do is take on a case you don't know how to handle. The best thing you can do? Refer them to someone who will make you look good. Someone who will do a great job for the client. In the client's mind, it adds value to you as the referral source.

Now the client knows you can always help them, and they can depend on you for any legal problem, and so can people in their network. Simply by referring them to the right attorney, you become invaluable to that client.

Client care and knowing when to hand off a case are great ways to build credibility.

In the client's mind, if the lawyer knows how to do the work, they'll handle it. If they don't, they've got someone in their corner who can. Either way, the client knows they're in good hands, and they'll always stay with you. That's the point.

Successful rainmaking begins with relationships. When you show up with integrity, communicate well, and take great care of both the client and the referral source, people will want to send business your way. Do that consistently, and referrals will become the engine that grows and sustains your practice.

CHAPTER 8

TURNING CLIENTS INTO ADVOCATES

In criminal defense, keeping a book of business—equivalent to a civil attorney's book—is difficult, mainly because, ideally, your clients don't reoffend. You're hoping they never need you again, although if people in their networks do, they'll call.

But here's the thing: Your client is still a critical referral source. If you did a great job for them, if they appreciated you, if their family liked you, they're going to remember you. And when someone they know gets into trouble, they'll send that person your way.

I once took on a federal case in another part of the country. It was a good case, and the client got a great result and was really happy. I had spent a lot of time with him and his family. He ended up telling someone else in jail about me, a person who had a much more serious case in the same courthouse. It was a big deal. That guy ended up hiring me, too.

So, then I was back in court with the same prosecutor. I remember when I showed up for the second case, he laughed and said, "So are you planning to take all the cases away from the attorneys out here?" And I joked, "What are the odds a lawyer from So Cal would get back-to-back cases out here?" The prosecutor smiled and said, "Well, the first guy must have liked you."

That's the point. Clients, when you treat them right, can open the door to a whole lot of future work, even in places you never expect. So, when people ask, "How do you grow your practice?" I always say, "Keep your clients happy."

FOLLOW UP

Often, I'll reach out to a former client after their probation has ended to discuss clearing their criminal record. It helps them with employment, and if needed, with professional licenses and immigration. It's helpful to the client and keeps us in touch.

As I've explained in depth, when someone refers a client to you, thank them with something they'll appreciate. It doesn't have to be extravagant, but it should be meaningful, and sometimes the right words are all you need.

As I mentioned in Chapter 7, the real key is staying in touch; you convey to your referral sources not only that you appreciate the business they send you, but also that the relationship is important to you. But just as critical is doing an outstanding job with the referrals you do get, both in results and in how you care for them. Because nothing is worse than if my friend sends a case, and the client calls him and says, "I can never get a hold of Bob." That makes both my friend and me look bad, and it will be the end of his referrals.

So, if you want to grow your base and your practice, you've got to take care of the people already in your orbit. That's how it grows. The more people you take care of, the more your name is out there, and the more it starts to come back to you.

Just recently, on a Sunday, someone walked into my office. I asked how they heard about me, and they said, "Some guy, I think he heard about you from someone else." So now I'm trying to figure out who referred them, because I want to thank them. And that's the point. The bigger your base gets, the harder it occasionally becomes to track who referred a particular case to you; and that's, of course, a good problem to have. But do everything you can to figure out who made that referral, and be sure to thank them.

Everything we've talked about so far, referrals, relationships, and doing quality work, is about growing your base. As you do, your job also includes staying in touch with those people.

ANSWER THE PHONE

I still have an "office" phone number, but I haven't verbally given it to clients in years. It's on my business card, along with my cell, but I tell everyone, clients, judges, clerks, "just call my cell." I literally do not have a desktop phone any longer. The office number rings to a service.

One thing I've come to learn over the years is that a big part of any attorney's job is to reduce a client's stress and anxiety. And one of the best ways I can do that is by being reachable. I mean, what's worse than being charged with a crime and not being able to get a hold of your lawyer? So, everyone gets my personal cell phone number.

Back in the 1990s, sure, I had a landline phone that sat on my desk. But now, I have one phone: my personal cell, and that's what I give out. I always tell clients they should feel free to call me whenever they need to. They are scared, they're in trouble, they want to know what I'm doing to help them, and they need to be able to reach me. So, I make it clear that no matter how often they call, even if it's on weekends, it's fine. I'm never too busy to talk with them.

Everyone has my cell number. And the reality is, when referral sources, clients, and potential clients can reach you directly, whether by text or call, without having to go through a gatekeeper, it's a much better experience.

Have you ever considered your relationship with referral sources, clients, and potential clients to be "experiences" for them? Why wouldn't you? You want them to have a positive experience because you have empathy for them, and you want them to speak positively about you to others, especially the person who sent them.

So, as part of the good experience, you want clients to be able to easily reach you when they need to. It especially helps when clients are professionals like doctors and lawyers, or people whose time is valuable. The last thing they want is to have to jump through several hoops simply to reach you. Giving them your cell shows that you have respect for their time and enhances your relationship.

Now, let's say I'm having a busy day. Maybe I'm driving or in court, not at my computer, and a new client calls. I still want to give them great service by spending enough time with them to properly begin our relationship. So, I need to quickly figure out how urgent it is, and whether they need me to intake them right now, or if I can schedule it for a little later that day.

First question I ask: "When's your court date?" Second, I ask, "When did this happen?" Based on their answers, the urgency in their voice, who referred them, and years of experience, I can usually tell right away whether we need to have the intake call right then, or soon thereafter, when I am better able to take notes and pay attention to what they're saying.

If I think they can be patient for the onboarding call, I'll say, "Would you mind if I call you back in a couple of hours? I'd rather wait until I'm in front of my computer so I can take proper notes and we don't have to repeat things later." That kind of comment builds trust, and then I make sure to call back exactly when I said I would. Potential clients must know you're reliable.

Texts are handled the same way as calls. If someone texts, "I'm a potential new client, sent by so-and-so," and I'm available, I'll text them right back: "Can I call you now?" If one of us is unavailable, I'll text to let them know I'll call as soon as possible. That's the real power of giving out your cell—it gives people confidence that they'll quickly hear back from you.

You might think giving out your cell phone number will lead to people abusing the privilege. But in all the years I've given it out, I've literally had one person call in the middle of the night. When people trust and respect you, in my experience, you don't have to spell out boundaries.

If you treat people well, they return the favor. I've literally never had to say, "Don't call me at night" or "Don't call me on weekends." And when people do call on a weekend, it's rare, and it's usually something truly urgent, or quick and basic. More often, they'll text.

It all comes down to the relationship. When clients know you care about them, they don't want to take advantage of your time—they return your respect. They assume I like to have evenings and weekends to myself. But honestly, the reason they don't call during those off hours is that they're so well informed of what is happening with their case, and nothing is truly urgent.

I always keep clients on top of what is happening with their cases. They know what's in the police reports, what the video shows, what the prosecutor has offered them to settle the case, my views on what we can do to get the very best offer, and they know what will happen next time in court. They know everything possible is being done to help them. They're not lying awake wondering, *Is the judge going to put me in jail tomorrow*?

Now, once in a while, I'll get a weekend call like, "My husband was just arrested," or "My daughter just got picked up." That's different. That's a new client, and of course, I want those calls at any time, and I'll call them back right away.

But here's the bigger point: When your clients are satisfied, informed, and respected, they don't unnecessarily try to contact you.

Many clients have told me just how much they appreciate that they can always reach me. The funny part is when I tell other lawyers I give out my personal cell, and it's on my card, they say, "How do you sleep at night? Don't people bother you all the time?" Nope.

Any inconvenience from getting the occasional weekend or late-night message is tiny compared to the value it brings my clients and the trust it builds. They feel supported, which calms them and makes them more confident in the process, plus it makes my job easier.

That's the power of being available. And when you're just getting started in your own practice, it sets you apart from other attorneys and makes you attractive to referral sources.

When you give people your cell, you send the signal that you're accessible, and it builds trust. Clients appreciate it. They tell other people, "You know what? My lawyer actually took my call on a Saturday." That turns into more referrals.

If you do your job well and keep clients informed, weekend calls should be rare. But when they happen, they won't be a burden. They'll be worth your time. They'll build your practice in ways answering services and office voicemail systems never can.

At the end of the day, building a thriving practice is about taking exceptional care of the people who trust you at one of the most stressful moments of their lives. When you treat clients with respect, communicate clearly, stay accessible, and continue nurturing those relationships long after the case is closed, they don't just remember you—they become your advocates. And those advocates will quietly, consistently, and powerfully help grow your business.

CHAPTER 9

SCALING SMART

Bringing on quality individuals to help with my practice has been a game-changer. I've been very lucky to bring people in who always stay with me for a long time. My last assistant was with me for over seven years. She was a great legal assistant, and I really valued her presence in the office. She made my life so much easier. When she decided she wanted to follow her dream in a different industry, although I was a bit sad for myself, I fully supported her.

She wasn't always slammed with work, so whenever she was not busy with firm work, she could study for her new profession in the office while on the clock. And you know what? She's opened up an entirely new client base by introducing me to people in her new profession, and she is one of my closest friends.

That's the kind of value great staff brings. It's not just about the tasks they handle day-to-day. It's about trust. It's about relationships. It's about the long-term benefit of having good people around you who grow with your practice.

So, when you're thinking about hiring someone to help you run your office, ask yourself:

- Can I trust this person?
- Will they represent me well?
- Will they grow with the practice?

This is what really matters, and if you've hired well, they're worth it. Hiring an attorney, though, comes with an entirely different set of risks.

SCALING YOUR BUSINESS

In criminal defense, scaling your business is hard. It's different from other types of law because you're in court so much. You make significantly more court appearances than other lawyers.

Let's say you make a bad paralegal or attorney hire in a personal injury firm. What's the worst that might happen? Maybe some interrogatories don't get done on time. Maybe they're not as thorough as you'd like. Maybe a deposition gets missed or rescheduled. Maybe you get sanctioned a little. But most of those things are fixable, and they're unlikely to embarrass you in front of the client.

Now compare that to criminal defense. You're in court constantly. The stakes are higher. If your associate doesn't show up and the client was told they don't need to be there, a warrant will be issued for their arrest. Other times, the client is sitting right there in court, listening, watching, and judging their attorney. If something goes wrong, if your associate is unprepared, if they treat the client badly, you can't hide it. The client might complain to the judge. They might go straight to the referral source and complain, "Why did you send me to that lawyer?" All are huge risks.

That's why, in criminal defense, you must protect your brand every day, especially when another attorney is out there representing you and your reputation. Yes, it matters in other areas of law, too, but it's so much easier to recover from mistakes when they don't play out in open court or directly with the client.

That's one reason it's said criminal defense lawyers never retire early. It's just harder to scale. Building a bigger firm usually means hiring other lawyers. And in this field, bringing someone in to work on cases you worked hard to get comes with huge risks to your reputation.

Now, if you don't care much about your brand, or if you're just not as protective of it as I am, then maybe you can scale faster. You can hire someone, take on more cases, and be okay with the risk. But me? I care about it. I've spent nearly forty years building my reputation, and I'm proud of what I've built. I'm not going to risk it because someone I hired didn't show up to court on time and forgot to let the clerk know.

ALL ABOUT ADMIN

What type of admin do you need when you set up shop? It includes necessary tasks like opening and closing files, coordinating the delivery of closed files to storage, and obtaining discovery from the other litigants. Discovery needs to be indexed and placed in your case management system.

There are basic office tasks too, like copying, printing, scanning, and ordering supplies, to name a few. And honestly, you don't need to spend a fortune to hire someone to do them. That said, you do want to find someone you trust, someone reliable, and who'll stick around.

If you don't give out your cell phone, at a minimum, you need someone to answer the phones, too. A receptionist might be an option, an answering service another. I've found both to be expensive. To save a few bucks, more lawyers are using overseas-based answering services.

These companies hire receptionists based overseas, where wages are lower. Once you open your doors, you'll want to weigh the cost of the service that best suits the amount and types of calls you expect to receive versus the cost of having someone in your office answer them.

A couple of friends do their own admin, and honestly, I think it takes too much time away from other things they could be doing to increase revenue. I don't want to overspend, but having someone else do it, whose hourly rate is lower than mine, frees me up to spend more time on tasks that make the firm money, such as working up my cases and networking—two critical duties of a rainmaker.

To make things run smoothly and to prevent legal issues, we created an employee and HR handbook. I have a friend who is an employment attorney, and with his help, it was easy and free to put it together. The guide is important because it outlines everything from how to hire and fire employees to step-by-step processes for day-to-day tasks.

The employee and HR handbooks explain how to open and close a file and order supplies, and they cover almost every potential question an employee might have. When we bring someone on, we give them the handbook right away. We don't expect them to memorize it overnight, but we do ask them to read through it over time so they can get familiar with how things work. You'll want to do the same, not only to save you time, but potentially to help you avoid any expensive problems with employees.

The value of having a great team? Let's say I'm going on vacation for a week. Do you think I'm stressed about it? Not at all. Because I know and trust everything's covered.

Here's another tip, especially for new lawyers, that applies no matter your area of law: Consider working in a suite with other lawyers. Where I work, the other lawyers do not handle criminal cases, and because I see them every day, they are natural referral partners.

Remember, you've got to figure out how you're going to handle marketing, networking, phone calls—all the things to build your brand—even before you begin working your caseload. The more work you can confidently delegate, the better. It's worth the expense.

THE ART OF DELEGATING LEGAL WORK

Meeting with clients, devising and managing a strategy for the case, conducting discovery, legal research, preparing documents, communicating with opposing counsel, negotiating, and making court appearances are just some of the tasks required in a typical case.

Even if you are able to hand off your admin, once you start scaling your firm, it will become difficult, if not impossible, to do what is required to ensure your client gets a great result while at the same time continuing to network and do the things necessary to grow.

The question becomes, which, if any of these tasks, can be delegated either to a less costly attorney, or paralegal, or should you do it yourself? The answer is different for everyone, and it is personal. It involves how much you want to work, to what extent you want to scale, and the value you place on having a life outside of work.

We'd all agree that certain tasks cannot be handed off to a non-attorney. Negotiating legal fees, representing a client in court, giving legal advice, making tactical decisions, and settling cases require professional judgment and constitute the practice of law. So, if you're busy enough and you want to get some help with these tasks, as we discussed earlier, you can bring in an attorney, give them a percentage, teach them your culture, and hope they do a good job with the clients, much as you would, so the referral sources remain happy.

There are other types of legal work you can assign to a paralegal. Scheduling, managing files, legal research, drafting certain types of legal documents, writing file reports, interviewing witnesses, and summarizing documents are some of those.

One interesting concern is what effect AI will have on delegating paralegal tasks. (See more of my thoughts about AI later in the chapter.) There will always be a need for an attorney's strategic decision-making in legal work. What AI can do, though, is quickly go through vast amounts of documents, look for certain information, and summarize it. These can include writings and even audio and video recordings.

AI can also tremendously speed up legal research by taking a prompt and efficiently going through statutes and cases to find what you're looking for. Then, the paralegal is needed simply to review the AI-generated product for accuracy.

With this technology, the need to delegate paralegal duties is reduced because those tasks can now be quickly completed by you. It literally may not make economic sense to spend a lot of money hiring someone to do this type of work since you can do it so quickly by yourself. That's a question you'll answer based on your personal and professional goals.

If the prompt is something like, "What's the statute of limitations on bear hunting in Montana in February?" AI will give you a direct answer in just a few seconds. If I need a 200-page deposition summarized, there are specific AI-based platforms that will spit out a page-line summary in a minute. What used to take three or four hours now takes minutes, even when you double-check the critical material. Just a few years ago, a lawyer or paralegal had to sit down and read every line and summarize it by hand, and they had to be paid. Now, AI and you can do it in seconds.

The point is, when you are getting started, think about your needs and stay lean. Then, as you scale, stay lean but get the help you need. You have all sorts of options.

HIRING OTHER ATTORNEYS

You know things are going well with your new firm when, driving home from the office late one Saturday afternoon, you sigh and think, *Sheesh, maybe I should just hire someone to help me so I don't have to work so many weekends.*

It's hard to get rich doing criminal defense, but one of the ways you can do it is by hiring another attorney and assigning them the cases you don't want to work on. It frees you up to bring in more of the types of cases you want to work on, and you don't need to turn as much away.

I don't follow this strategy. I'd rather focus on bringing in the types of cases I want to work on and not concern myself with the issues surrounding employing attorneys. In other words, I prefer to bring in fewer but better cases, not more cases, where I need attorney help.

But adding employees is one way people try to scale. And maybe it's worth expanding on, because honestly, adding low-cost employees is how to scale in most any industry. So, if that's the path you want, that's okay.

But here's the thing: When you hire another attorney, their values and yours absolutely must align.

There's nothing worse than working for years to establish a reputation as an attorney who is always on time for a court appearance, and then one day, receiving a call from the clerk asking where your associate is. The associate should also be really good at handling cases, especially if they're not a rainmaker. Because if they're not bringing in business, then they better be great at representing you, to your referral sources, new clients, and in court.

So, how do you know when it's the right time to bring someone new on board? I'd say the obvious answer is: When the amount of work you have exceeds the amount of time you want to spend on it. That could mean a few things.

I already mentioned that I like working on a certain kind of case with a certain kind of client. So, the goal, for me, has always been to take fewer cases that pay better. It makes sense when you're solo. But if you bring in an associate, you have the option to take on more cases, even the types you may not want to work on, and maybe at a lower rate, because someone else will put in the time. That's just how you scale any business.

But here's where the pitfalls show up. As a solo practitioner, you are your brand. That brand is what your referral sources, clients, and people in the court system associate with your name. So, when you bring in someone else, they, along with you, become the face of your practice. And that can either help or hurt your brand—the one you've spent years growing. (I'll talk more about the importance of your brand later in this chapter.)

You have to think it through before you hire an attorney. On the one hand, you can make the conscious choice to go through your career on your own. You'll make less money, but you control the workflow and your brand image.

On the other hand, you never know how someone will work out. They could be fantastic—work hard, buy into your brand, have a desire to become your partner someday—in other words, a great hire. Or, they may not do things the way you want them done. They may not follow up the way you would. They may not return calls as quickly. They may do things to disappoint your clients and referral sources. They may not care about the things you care about because they're not as invested as you are in the firm's success.

So, the real question when hiring isn't just: Can they do the job? In my view, the concern should also be: Will they represent the brand I've spent years building? And no matter how well you think you hit the hire, you just never know.

STAYING INVOLVED AFTER THE HIRE

Once the new attorney is on board, your job isn't done. You can't just set it and forget it after three months. You've got to stay plugged in. You should be checking in with your referral sources. You should walk into court and ask the bailiffs, the clerks, even the judges, "Hey, how's it going with so-and-so from my office?" Are they showing up on time? Are they treating clients and the court with respect? Are they doing things the way you would?

As an employer, you can't be afraid to ask those questions. You have to stay involved. Most importantly, it's not just about following up with the courts. You've got to check in with the people who send you business. The worst-case scenario is hearing from a referral source that your associate or paralegal dropped the ball with a client, especially when the person trusted you enough to send you a client in the first place.

When someone you hired makes the court, and your referral sources unhappy, you're stuck figuring out how to undo the damage. You may have to reach out to the referral source and say, "I'm sorry that happened. From now on, I'll personally handle any case you send." You may have to walk into a courtroom and apologize to a clerk or a judge and say, "That's not how we operate, and I'll make sure it doesn't happen again."

So, an attorney hire may be the best thing that ever happened to your practice, and judges, clerks, clients, and referral sources all like them. But as you can see, the opposite can occur, too, and your brand might take a hit. You're the only person who can repair it, and it takes time and effort away from working on your cases. That's the risk. So, when you're thinking about hiring another lawyer, make sure you're ready to stay involved and on top of everything they touch. Keep a close eye on your practice every day. Because your reputation is everything.

A WORD ABOUT AI AND THE LEGAL LANDSCAPE

A lot of people believe that no matter what happens with AI, there's always going to be a need for lawyers. And it's true—to a point. AI can't go into court and argue a case. AI can't stand before a jury or a judge and deliver a closing argument. AI can't actually be a lawyer.

That said, AI is already doing some of the work lawyers used to do. For example, some attorneys are cheating and using AI to write their briefs. And judges are starting to catch on. As far as I understand it, the question is: Are judges somehow able to detect whether something was written by AI? And when the answer is yes, you will see the judge become very angry on the bench.

If you're a first- or second-year lawyer just getting started, AI is likely taking a lot of your job description away from you. If your tasks are research and writing, AI can already do a big chunk of that, instantly. And it gets more accurate every day.

The possibility exists that a decade from now, the only lawyers left in big firms may be the partners—the people at the top who bring in the business—because everyone else will be replaceable. You won't need an associate when you are able to research the answer you need in a few minutes.

I used to believe the legal profession was pretty insulated and that it would always need a human touch. But now I realize AI might actually be removing the need for younger attorneys, at least in traditional law firm roles.

Let's say I'm a partner at a firm, and I've got an opening for an associate. The job used to require someone who could research, write well, and put together solid briefs. If they brought in clients, great. That was a bonus, but it wasn't required.

Now, with AI, I can do the research and write the brief myself.

YOUR BRAND AND HIRING

Why is your new firm's brand important? It is your message to potential referral sources and clients, it creates trust, and differentiates you from other attorneys who do similar work. How do you decide on a brand? Think about the types of clients you are targeting. In my case, clients who are invested in their lives—family, home, job, reputation, money in the bank, people for whom a criminal conviction and jail time are simply not an option.

You must also explain why you are a better value than your competitors. It can start with you being a great listener, that you show empathy for your clients and their situations, and how you will get them through a difficult time in their lives with a minimum of stress and anxiety. A key is being able to define your brand in a single sentence when it's time to stand up in a networking meeting and tell others in twenty seconds what you do. Be able to succinctly tell your audience what you do and how you can help them.

When starting your law firm, the first thing you must decide on and understand is your brand because every business decision you make must align with it. Think about that for a second. When you're just starting out on your own, one of the biggest decisions you'll make is who to hire, whether it's an admin, a paralegal, or another attorney. Whoever it is should fit the culture and the environment you're trying to create. If the question is, "What do you have to know to scale?" the takeaway is, "your brand." It's going to guide you on who to hire.

Your brand will also shape the empathy and approach you bring to potential clients and referral sources. Once you're clear on your brand and what's behind it, you'll see how it influences everything, who you hire, how you communicate, and how you build relationships with referral sources, clients, and even courts.

Decisions on how to grow your firm center on the trust you build with clients and referral sources, and your ability to explain why you bring tremendous value for the fees you charge. In turn, these decisions require you to know your brand and what you're actually trying to accomplish.

FILLING THE SPOTS

In my experience, word-of-mouth has always been the best way to find new hires. Networking groups can also help with staffing, given that you are around a group of people you've come to know and trust. Oftentimes, they may be a good source of information regarding a potentially solid hire who is looking, or has recently become available.

If you don't have a large network, there are apps and software platforms designed to forward good applicants to you. The screening process can be tailored to your needs. In addition, if a big law firm has a round of layoffs, its former support staff may be available.

I'm not saying to poach anyone, but if people have left, or your friends know someone? Reach out. Canvas your network. Ask around. This is a time to be selfish. The bottom line? Hire the person who best fits your brand and whom you can afford. Your goal is for your staff to grow with you.

Legal staffing firms are another option. I know someone who recently hired a strong assistant through such a firm. Initially, the individual remains the employee of the staffing firm, and you pay the firm for a certain number of months. If you like the person, you can then hire them permanently, after making some sort of financial arrangement with the firm.

I've never hired anyone this way, but it's probably not a bad idea. At least you get a relatively risk-free chance to see their work quality and whether they're a fit for your brand. In some ways, it's actually safer than hiring them as a full-time employee right off the bat. Try them out for as long as you need. If you really like them, you can go ahead and hire them.

Growing a practice isn't just about more clients—it's about hiring the right people and making sure they uphold your standards. Delegation only works if the people you trust represent you well in front of clients, referral sources, and the courts.

Hire carefully, delegate wisely, and stay engaged. The right team can help you grow—the wrong one can undo years of work.

CHAPTER 10

WORK, LIFE, AND THE BUSINESS OF BALANCE

We've talked about what it takes to be successful professionally, but if your personal life isn't great, if the time away from home is a problem, none of it really matters. It's the age-old question: Do you live to work, or work to live? My goal early on was the latter, but it surely felt like the former for many years while I was growing.

But once I had a stable number of referral sources, I was making more money in my own practice than I would have at a firm, and living a better life because I could take the cases I wanted and come and go as I pleased. The only person I had to answer to? Me. Not a partner in a corner office who was profiting off the sweat of my labor.

Since you're reading this book, then you, too, have likely realized the best way to financial and personal freedom is to become an entrepreneur. Law firm downsizing and the rise of AI illustrate the new reality. Think about it. Does working at a law firm, or even switching firms, seem to be the way to financial and personal independence, or more likely, will you be forced to sacrifice some of your goals to keep your job, which you can barely tolerate? Why *did* you go to law school?

It takes several years to successfully build your own practice while at the same time becoming a rainmaker. It takes patience and lots of hard work, especially as you grow.

THE PRESSURE COOKER

The amount of time spent on your practice is one problem; stress is another. Daily, lawyers face immense pressure and difficult decisions. If you decide to leave your firm and go out on your own, or start fresh after you've been let go, you'll add layers and layers of work on top of your everyday job to become the best lawyer you can be.

And if you don't plan ahead—if you don't think things through—the stress of your job and time away from home can cost you the things that matter most. Your marriage. Your family. Your health. Your relationships. Your career.

The fundamental changes in the legal profession are partially to blame. Things like the streamlining of large and mid-size law firms since the pandemic, the difficulty fired lawyers have in finding anything other than another dead-end job at some other law firm, and the resignation of attorneys who realize when they woke up one day, they'll never make equity partner, and are stuck. All of these situations are stressful.

To owe tens, if not hundreds of thousands of dollars in student loans, and then to wake up one day knowing you're maxed out at your firm, and dependent on others for your living, must be a bad feeling, given the uncertainty it creates. It is stressful not knowing how to improve your situation when you've never been taught, especially when the thought of starting your own firm seems daunting.

For lawyers transitioning to their own practices, the obvious stress is ensuring their income exceeds expenditures. They don't want to work themselves to the bone for an income large enough to cover the mortgage, the two car payments, the kids' education, retirement contributions, and the occasional vacation.

The stress of practicing law is acute and growing. Too much work, deadlines, working on cases not really in your area of expertise, the pressure of needing to be hired when a potential client walks in the door, being available 24/7/365, networking, learning new technology, whether to be remote, office expenses—this is what we face every single day of our careers. And after a while, despite their best intentions, some attorneys simply can't deal with it. And it's okay.

There is a mental health crisis in the legal world, and the threat of burnout to lawyers new to their own practices is real. A variety of surveys show more than one-half of all lawyers suffer from anxiety, more than one-third have depression, even more feel isolated, and one-fifth have contemplated suicide. Think about that. When you are among your attorney friends or at a conference, think about those sheer numbers.[3]

And all those mental health issues must also affect the quality of the attorney's work product.

What does this stress look like? Difficulty sleeping, irritation, trouble staying focused, pulling away from friends and family, detachment and disengagement, procrastination, unhealthy eating habits, avoiding exercise, increasing alcohol consumption, and abuse of drugs that help you sleep, even illegal drugs.[3]

It's not just the job itself. It's all the other pressure that comes with it. Think about it. Trying to grow a practice, do quality work, keep your marriage alive, stay close to your kids, maintain your friendships, be *present* at the dinner table—it's a lot. And they don't teach you this in law school. They don't teach it anywhere.

These figures and the underlying concerns are alarming. If you feel you're starting to go down one of these rabbit holes, there are

---

3 Lita Abella, "Wellness Strategies for Mental Health Issues Among Attorneys and Legal Professionals," *California Lawyers Association*, September 29, 2022, https://calawyers.org/california-lawyers-association/wellness-strategies-for-mental-health-issues-among-attorneys-and-legal-professionals/

resources for you to access, and your State Bar offers counselors and support. And I bet at least one person came to mind when you read these statistics. Maybe you even saw yourself. If you're even close to any of these concerns, this is your wake-up call.

The point is, if you're building an empire, you've got to be sure you're also carving out time for yourself and the people you love because none of it matters if you lose them, or yourself.

When making decisions about cases you bring in, and whether to hire, whatever it may be regarding your law firm, you must be intentional and think through the effects your business decisions will have on your mental health. You're no good to anyone if making more money sends you over a cliff.

Ideally, you want to integrate becoming a rainmaker with staying physically and emotionally healthy. And you can make room for it all. Here's what worked for me:

- Alone time
- Time with family
- Time with friends

In addition, show yourself some love. If you enjoy fantasy football, playing poker with your buddies, riding dirt bikes, or swimming, build those activities into your schedule. Don't take on too much work. If you have, excise that work in the order of least importance.

Most lawyers are very competitive, so you can channel it into playing in a lawyer's softball or basketball league. Ride a bike or run on the weekends, and every so often, run a 5K. If you love cars, take the time to enjoy a car show, or if you live near a race track, take your cool ride over there so you can race it full speed down the track.

And if you find yourself feeling that the stress of the job might be getting to you, talk to someone. Get some help. It is not embarrassing; people won't feel sorry for you. In fact, you may help them realize they have the same problems. Once you start down the path of drinking, drugs, isolation, or anger, it's much harder to get healthy.

The point is, you need an outlet. Something just for you. Not for your spouse, not for your kids, not for your clients, just for you. Where you're not constantly giving or performing. Where you get to recharge and enjoy the moment. Where you get to be a little selfish. It's perfectly okay.

FINDING FULFILLMENT OUTSIDE THE OFFICE

What "personal success and fulfillment" looks like evolves over your career. What matters in year two is different from what matters in year ten. It's definitely different as I approach year forty.

When I first went out on my own, I probably worked sixty to eighty hours a week. I had to make sure my clients were getting my best legal work, but I also had to grow the practice, go to events, and build relationships. All of that took time away from things I enjoyed.

Back when I was in high school, I wasn't the guy out chasing girls every weekend. I was part of a group of guys who all worked at Naugles Restaurant, sort of like Del Taco. Instead of going out, we played poker every Friday night. I was seventeen years old, playing poker until three in the morning, then heading over to get breakfast burritos after. We did that for years.

Somewhere along the way, I actually became a pretty good poker player. So, it didn't stop there. When I got to law school, I kept playing. I used to go to some of the casinos in Gardena, a suburb of Los Angeles. These were legitimate casinos, not home games, and I played poker to help pay for law school. I could win $50 a session eight out of ten times. I wasn't getting rich, but it helped cover school expenses. And while I was playing at the casino, for a couple of bucks, I could get dinner. When you're a broke law student, that's a great deal.

Before my daughter was old enough to start her softball career, even after becoming a lawyer, I played a lot of poker. It was both a stress reliever and a money-maker. I was good at it. I used to drive from Orange County to Commerce Casino near downtown Los Angeles three times a week to play the 10-20-40 Hold'em game. I could also beat it eight out of ten times. The money I won went toward nice things for the house, trips, and whatever came up.

Playing all that poker over the years had an amazing impact on my law career. I developed the ability to read people. If you can tell the hand they're holding in poker, you might use those same skills in reading another lawyer or a judge. Crazy but true.

I remember one time playing in a tournament with over 800 players and winning. It was something like $50,000! Back in the early 2000s, I even played in the Main Event of the World Series of Poker, which was broadcast on ESPN. The tournament started out with 2,800 players, and I made it all the way to the fourth day when they were down to the last 150!

One of my favorite stories about the tournament was, I hadn't planned on playing for so many days, and when I called my office each day to check in and say "I'm still in the tournament!!" my assistant said, "Don't worry about a couple of upcoming court appearances, have fun and win," and she'd get them covered. Talk about fun. And my assistant made it all the better by getting the court matters covered.

You can't start a new practice, thinking you'll be wine-tasting every month or heading to Vegas every weekend. That's just not how it works. You're going to work evenings. You're going to work Saturdays. You have to deliver great work, keep clients happy, and build a reputation. Just as important, you have to put in networking time and keep those golden referral sources happy. That's your foundation. And once that's solid, the time and lifestyle you sacrificed will return.

For the first five or six years, you should expect your quality of life to take a back seat to getting your practice off the ground. You'll still have a good life, but your law practice sets up the rest of your life. It will determine how much you'll need to work later, what kind of income you'll earn, and what kind of freedom you'll have. It even helps shape your social network.

I still squeezed in some poker here and there. But real vacations? I probably went three years without taking more than two or three days off. I'd go with my brother to fish in Cabo, or go to Vegas, but just for a couple of days, nothing crazy. That's just what I had to do to unwind. The hours were a sacrifice my family made for the business, but unlike working for someone else at a law firm, I knew it would pay off, and it did.

If someone tells you they built a successful practice working thirty or forty hours a week in the early years, I'd question it. You could be marginally successful, but probably not the way you want to be. Just remember, much of the initial effort required to become a rainmaker is temporary. It will get better over time as your base grows.

By my fifth or sixth year, I could take a trip for five or six days and feel confident someone in my network could cover my practice. If I had a simple hearing, not a trial, I could pay another attorney to handle it, for example, if the purpose of the hearing was just to choose new dates. I had relationships with young, capable lawyers who were happy to handle routine matters for a modest fee.

The support of my network, not just in sending business, but helping me not stress while away on a trip, was really valuable. I wouldn't worry about a short court appearance in the middle of a vacation. I could stay an extra day or two without it throwing my whole practice off. I'd explain to my clients what was happening, and because I did so, they were always fine with it.

Even then, though, I'd still get client and referral source calls while I was gone. I always gave out my cell. And yes, I'd always answer it. Before I left on the trip, I emailed everyone:

"I'm going on vacation for a week. If it's urgent, call me. If it can wait, I'd appreciate it. No matter what, I'm here to help, so don't hesitate to let me know if you need something."

And most people respected my judgment that it was okay to take a vacation. But potential new clients also called. Obviously, they hadn't seen the email. They needed immediate help and reassurance, and I wasn't going to lose them just because I was on a beach. And I thought it was really a good sign for my firm to bring in a new case while I was out of the country.

I was able to onboard new clients over the phone, connect with them emotionally and legally, and either schedule something for when I got back or get another attorney to cover if something urgent needed attention. Clients appreciated it. They felt cared for and prioritized, even if I wasn't physically there. That's what people want, and that is what you have to be able to do to enjoy your life and become a rainmaker.

A key to making this lifestyle work as I continued to grow was the great team I had assembled back at the office. I remember once being in Cabo. A new client called about a case where something had to be filed while I was still going to be down there. My staff knew how to handle it because they were trained to file the correct Substitution of Attorney forms or coordinate with a lawyer next door if something more was needed. Talk about peace of mind. Even though I was the only lawyer in my office, I wasn't the only person keeping the practice going.

You don't take the first week away until you're truly ready—until you have confidence in your systems, your staff, and your network. But you are on your way!

Most attorneys don't work in isolation. You're in an office or on a floor with other lawyers. Build relationships with them. I recently went to Nashville, and while I was gone, a last-minute court appearance came up on a new matter. A workers' comp lawyer on my floor, someone who's never done a private criminal case, stepped up to cover the appearance.

I gave him a script; every single word he needed to say to the judge, and I mentioned to him that if it went south, he was to simply tell the judge I was on vacation, and to continue the matter a week until I got back, which I knew the judge would agree to. "Your honor, the client enters a plea of not guilty, denies all the special allegations, reserves all motions, and asks for a pretrial on August 5, and we waive the right to a speedy trial." He read it almost word for word, and five minutes after it was done, I was able to call the client and tell him everything was fine. Everyone was happy. Done. That's how it works.

It's a cop-out to say, "I can't go on vacation because no one can cover for me." There's always someone. You just have to plan for it. Your spouse and kids won't thank you for being the martyr. They'll appreciate you for showing up when it matters.

I remember when I started my firm, I thought about the trade-offs. I wasn't spending as much time at home, with my friends, and doing as many fun things on weekends as I would have liked. But I was building something bigger that would serve me for my entire career. The paradigm shift wasn't easy. But I knew if I did this right, I'd get something better in return. What made it better? I was working for me, not for someone else.

Sure enough, things got better. When my daughter was old enough to start sports, I was able to be there for her. This was because I owned my own firm, with no boss and no expectation to be in the office, since a partner was there. I was able to come and go as I pleased. When she had a game at 2 p.m. on a weekday, I could go. If she had a practice at 3:30, I could coach. No law firm would have allowed it. They want billable hours. They want you behind a desk. I was building something so I could be *present* in my family's lives.

That's one of the real benefits of owning your own practice. You work like crazy early on, but if you're smart, if you build systems, train your staff, treat people with empathy, and nurture your network, you earn flexibility. You earn freedom. And that's worth every hour I put in during those early years.

NO MORE NINE TO FIVE

You already knew this while working at a law firm, but one of the biggest benefits of being an entrepreneur is that you don't have to work nine to five. So long as you get done what needs to be done, you can make your own hours. Freedom opens the door to doing things that truly matter to you.

For me, it was coaching my daughter's softball teams. I started coaching when she was six years old and stayed involved until she started college. At one point, when she was in middle school, they even talked me into coaching the middle school team. That meant leaving work every day of the week at 1:00 p.m., running a 2:00 p.m. practice, and then heading back to the office by 4:00 p.m., oftentimes in my coaching gear. I could only do it because I worked for myself.

And the truth is, being able to make time for things I loved, like coaching her, made all the day-to-day work feel less like a grind. When you're doing something fun, everything balances.

There were two big reasons I loved coaching. One, as a former wannabe athlete myself, I've always believed youth coaches should be people who actually know the game and know how to teach it. Unfortunately, a lot of youth sports teams are coached by well-meaning parents who don't really have the skill set to help develop kids.

And two, I just loved baseball. I grew up a Dodgers fan. Now, I unfortunately follow the Angels, but I grew up going to games with my parents, and baseball stuck with me. When our daughter was two or three, we started taking her to Angels games. She loved it. She loved the atmosphere, nibbling on a hot dog, and watching the players. She had her favorite players by the time she was five or six.

So, when we started looking for a sport for our daughter to try, softball just made sense. It was similar enough to baseball and something we could enjoy together. Her mom is from Colombia, and while mom didn't grow up with baseball, she knew it and liked it, especially because there were a couple of Colombian players in the major leagues.

We signed our daughter up for the local youth league when she was five. I became her coach right away. We met a lot of great parents, and yeah, some classic helicopter parents too, but I loved coaching all the kids.

In the first season, she started off playing catcher. Then one day we needed a pitcher, so I said, "Get out there!" She liked it. That was the main thing. So, we started working with her, and by the time she was seven, she made the All-Star team, and I was the coach. Even at that age, practice was every day for two hours: 4:00 p.m. to 6:00 p.m. Do you think I could have signed on as a coach if I worked for someone else?

And if you are the parent of a pitcher, you know all the times, on top of practice, she had to throw—at least three times a week for years.

On weekends, we played tournaments all over Southern California—all day Saturday and Sunday, and even some holiday

Mondays. I remember one tournament where our seven-year-olds lost every single game. The parents were bummed, the kids were sad, and the coaches were, too. We had one tournament left that year in Rancho Bernardo, down in San Diego. After practice, I pulled the girls together and said, "Let's just go out and have fun at this next one. Don't worry about winning. Just have a blast!"

We went undefeated and won the tournament. One of our moms photographed the whole thing, including the final pitch, my daughter striking out the last batter to win it all.

My assistant coach and I were both intense dads. When she struck out the final batter to win the tournament, my assistant went running and jumping for joy out onto the field. All the girls and coaches followed him, jumping up and down, screaming like we'd just won the World Series. These girls were seven years old. The parents went crazy. It was one of those moments where I was just hooked, and I will never forget the last pitch, then the celebration.

The parents made a tunnel with their arms, and the players ran through it. Then they all got their trophies. For a seven-year-old, it was a big deal. Probably even more for the parents. That was the beginning of something really special. Unforgettable moments.

I coached her through the city league, through All-Stars, through fall ball. Even in high school, she played travel ball all over the country. I co-coached with friends, and we stuck with it all through high school. That's what opened the door for her to get recruited to play in college.

I can't even explain how close it made the two of us. We went together on a two-week college recruiting trip to New York, Boston, Rhode Island, and Pennsylvania. Another one-week trip just to Boston and Maine. We visited eight or nine schools on one trip. Another trip was to Minnesota, and even one to Northern California. I helped her write emails to college coaches, drove her to pitching and hitting lessons, and to the store for a new glove or bat.

It gave me a chance to talk to her about being a good student, being well-rounded, and doing volunteer work. It wasn't just softball, it was preparation for life—with all its ups and downs.

And it brought us together in a way nothing else ever could. If you're working at a firm, ask yourself, *Will the partners let you have a life like this with your children?* If not, by reading this book, you are gaining the tools to set your life up so you can do the things that *really matter*.

One of my favorite stories: my daughter was in fifth or sixth grade, and her class had the Sacramento trip, every California kid knows about it. You fly up mid-week in the morning, visit the Capitol and the railroad museum, have lunch, and fly home. It's a rite of passage.

Well, her team was in the city playoffs. She was our best pitcher. If she went on the Sacramento trip and stayed the whole day, she'd miss that night's semifinal game.

There was a very animated discussion at home the night before the game. I thought, "We need her to pitch." So, I flew up with her in the morning; we just did the Capitol, skipped the museum, and flew back in time for the game. She pitched. We won. That got us to the championship.

To this day, my daughter still teases me about it. It's a great father-daughter story.

The point of all the softball stories? Seriously, how many attorney dads can take two weeks off to go on college tours? Do you know many attorney dads who can be away from the law firm in the middle of the workday to coach? How many young attorneys, or attorneys new to starting their own practice, are comfortable not working weekends? Freedom.

Figure out when to get the work and networking done, and then enjoy your life, even if you are just starting up. That's one of the gifts of running your own business. There's no way I could've done it at a law firm. I had such a great team back at the office, and a good network of attorney friends who could handle anything unexpected that came up with a client or court. Those memories made all the extra time I put into work and networking worth it.

Coaching and traveling with my daughter weren't just good for her. They were good for me. They gave me a break. They reminded me why I worked so hard. When I got back to work, I felt better. More focused. More motivated. I knew why I had to get the work done and continue to grow my network. It was my "why."

And here's the thing: I've been out of the office during the work week a lot over the years. For something like thirty of the last thirty-two years, I've gone to Las Vegas with the same five college friends for March Madness. The only two times we missed were during the pandemic.

But here's the twist: During those years when my daughter had games, I'd still go to Vegas on Thursday, then get up at 4 a.m. on Saturday, drive back to Orange County, coach her game, and then immediately drive *back* to Vegas in time for Saturday night dinner with my friends. The parents thought I was nuts. My friends thought I was nuts. Even my daughter thought I was nuts.

But I wouldn't change a thing. Absolutely great memories.

And I'll never forget the last game she pitched in college. She played four years in college, and the pandemic began towards the beginning of her senior year. In her last game before the lockdown, she pitched great. Afterward, the coach said, "There's a chance this was our last game."

It *was* her last game.

College softball players write a kind of goodbye letter when they're done. I'll never forget what she wrote. She thanked her favorite coaches. She thanked her mom for driving her to lessons, for always being there. And then she thanked me.

She wrote, *"My dad will be more sad than me that I'm retired now."*

Wow, that was hard to read. In a good way. Because you know how kids don't usually post sappy stuff about their parents? But she did. And it was one of those things that made all the extra hours I had to spend with work worth it. The time, the money, the effort—everything.

All that softball, and all those college visits. All those late nights working on trial briefs in hotel rooms, getting up at 5:30 a.m. to go to the office so I had enough time to get my work done. All the weird hours, the sacrifice, it all came full circle. And I know someday she's going to tell her kids about the crazy stuff her dad did. I think she'll be that kind of attorney, too. She'll figure out how to make it all work so she has the work-life balance she wants.

You can make it work, too. You just have to decide what matters most, and then build your practice around it. You don't have to choose between your business and your life. In fact, I think your life is what gives your business purpose.

CHARITY WORK

Back in the 1960s, when I was in elementary school, I was always hustling for a few extra bucks. I'd wash my neighbor's cars for fifty cents. I had my bucket, hose, soap, sponge, and towel ready to go every Saturday morning at 8:00 a.m. At the time, a pack of baseball cards was a dime, and a triple-scoop ice cream cone was fifteen cents, so it was all good.

And back then, once a year, like clockwork, our mail carrier would deliver an envelope to our house from a well-known nonprofit that worked with at-risk youth. The letter told the charity's story and asked for a donation to help the children they worked with. My parents explained to me what the organization did, how they helped kids a lot less lucky than me, and encouraged me to donate as much of my car-wash money as I wanted. I remember, every year, giving five dollars of my own hard-earned bounty—a lot for a seven-year-old back then!

Fast forward to the early 2000s, a friend of mine was in a networking group about fifty miles away. I checked into it and decided it was worth a look—the other members were professionals who could send the types of clients I liked working with, and I had the bandwidth to do it.

I drove up for a meeting and was impressed with the people involved. But the guy running the group said, "You can only join if you're on the board of a nonprofit." He invited me back another day when ten nonprofits would be presenting. He said I could meet them all and pick one I liked. I was in a fortunate place in life, and it felt like the right time to give back. Little did I realize how life-changing the invitation would be.

When I came back, I met someone from a particular nonprofit, a really incredible organization that positively changes the lives of at-risk youth. At that time, the charity had expanded into California and was growing a local board of directors. They needed people who could help connect them with judges and probation officers in juvenile court, so they could build relationships and obtain referrals. Seemed like a great fit.

It was the same group who received some of my car-wash money when I was a kid—an unbelievable coincidence. Meeting the executive director triggered those good memories from my childhood in the 1960s. So, when I had the opportunity to connect with the same charity again as an adult, it felt like karma. I immediately said yes and joined the board, where I stayed for fourteen years. I helped raise lots of money, met a lot of impressive kids, and connected the charity with some people who were able to provide help to those same youth.

Every Christmas, our board members would buy gifts for the kids and ask friends and colleagues to contribute. One of us would dress up as Santa so the kids could have a real Christmas, something many of them had literally never experienced.

One year, I brought my daughter's Brownie troop to sing Christmas carols to some of the kids we were serving, literally babies, to eighteen-year-olds. The Brownies met the babies, some of whom had been abandoned, and sang for the older kids, many of whom had been through very hard times. I remember the experience well. It was incredibly moving for all of us.

Santa showed up, and there were hundreds of gifts. Each child we cared for received five or six high-quality presents, including bikes, PlayStations, and whatever else was popular. My daughter loved it. She started inviting her friends, and the troop sang year after year.

But in 2017, the nonprofit left California, and just like that, our board of seventeen people had no organization to support.

Instead of joining another board, three others and I decided to create our own foundation. We were now somewhat experienced in the ways of nonprofits, and we wanted to be different from a traditional charity. We'd raise money, set our own mission, and fund organizations we vetted and believed in.

The foundation partners with wineries from Napa, Sonoma, and Paso Robles, and the primary fundraiser is a unique wine-tasting event, literally next to the beach. A lot of money is raised and awarded to deserving nonprofits that align with the mission.

I've gotten very little work from either group. But that was never the goal. I did it because I genuinely wanted to. It felt like the right thing to do, especially given that I felt such a long-term connection to the first charity. But as a side benefit, it taught me a lot about empathy and, in the process, helped me understand the right way to treat others having trouble in their lives.

It's funny. I would be out there defending people accused of crimes one day, then the next day, I'd be raising money for at-risk youth. That kind of balance changes something inside you. Especially when you have kids of your own, it changes how you look at people who are not as fortunate as you. You realize how lucky you are to be in this profession and to be sitting on my side of the desk. It provides clarity on how you should treat people.

> **Here's the key: When you feel good about yourself, it's a lot easier to have empathy for others.**

If you're looking for a way to grow as a person and are passionate about a cause, especially something that helps you enjoy your time away from the office, being part of a board of directors is satisfying and will change your life for the better.

Of course, in your law practice, relationships and referrals matter, but joining a board and working hard to support the mission is really important, and people appreciate you. Some people want to protect animals. Some are passionate about helping at-risk youth. Others care deeply about the environment or about providing medical care to people who can't afford it.

Why is nonprofit work relevant to networking and business relationships? Well, I'll be the first one to tell you many people join boards because they think it makes them look good and enhances their resume, but then do little or nothing. Don't be that person. Applying your skill and talent to help raise money for those less fortunate than you is a great thing to do and leaves a lasting legacy for those who care about you.

What's interesting, though, is that for me, when I think about it, serving on both boards and really taking to heart the missions served to deepen my empathy. It has shaped who I am. For you, it will help you put into perspective how many of your business worries are really "first-world" problems that many others wish they had.

When I worked directly with children whose parents treated them horribly, abandoned them, left them for dead, abused them—it reinforced what really is important—treat people well and with respect. And in the business world, just like in the world of giving, empathy is an important part of who you are, what motivates you, and ultimately why people want to be around you. Empathy is critical to making clients, referral sources, and the courts happy. A giving mindset makes you not just a better lawyer, but a better human.

The irony of the story? I decided not to join the networking group.

AVOIDING BURNOUT

Your practice really breaks down into two main buckets. One is your practice, meaning the actual legal work required of you, as well as the networking necessary to achieve your goals. The second is administrative duties. And here's the thing: if you don't stay on top of the admin, it'll take over your whole practice. You'll be buried in it. You won't have time to do the marketing and legal work that actually brings in business or moves your cases forward.

If you're just starting your own practice, the goal should be to get help with the admin as soon as you can afford it. I mean it. Do it the minute you can.

If you can't afford too much, ask your spouse to help—your friend's high schooler who has some free time on weekends—even your middle school son or daughter can scan, copy, and file.

A great hire I've made is my senior paralegal/office manager. We've been working together for over a decade, and she's the anchor who keeps The Hartmann Law Firm running smoothly. She doesn't just help with cases; she handles a lot of the administrative work that would otherwise eat up my day. She manages payroll, employment matters, handles correspondence, and keeps our backend running. That frees me up to focus almost entirely on being a lawyer.

Because she is a paralegal, I try to give her as much paralegal-type work as is possible in a criminal defense firm: preparing standard discovery motions, corresponding with the DMV, reviewing police reports, summarizing videos, and other types of discovery. She is great, and it really helps me be efficient when handling my cases.

See the theme here? She's great. I value the quality of her work, her reliability, and her ability to put up with me, and I don't want to lose her. It is very difficult to find great help, much less a good person who is a perfect fit for the culture I've tried to establish.

So, I pay her what she's worth. As much as possible, I try to accommodate any particular needs she has. If she needs some time off, fine. If she needs to come in late or leave early every so often, it's not a problem. I also try to do something special for her every so often. She's a colleague, not merely a subordinate.

And given how busy we are, I also have an administrative assistant I've known since she was born, the daughter of a good friend. She fits our culture perfectly and does a great job by taking mundane administrative tasks out of my daily routine. In fact, she's so helpful, earlier this year, when a long trial caused me to miss some networking meetings, she acted as my substitute. The joke now is, the group likes her a lot more than me!

> **I can't emphasize this enough: If you're lucky enough to make a great hire, do what it takes to never let them get away.**

For me, burnout comes from admin, not legal work. So, if you've got someone who is really good at handling all the admin that goes with running your firm, you're way ahead of the next person. We've talked about the importance of spending time with clients and referral sources, staying in touch with them, networking, marketing, and doing a great job on your cases. None of it is possible if you're drowning in admin. And, a good assistant can help you stay in touch with your clients and referral sources.

The sooner you bring in someone good to help you out, the sooner you can focus on what only you can do: the legal work and networking. But to really scale, you'll need to be free of the admin duties, which can suck you down a rabbit hole. Someone else can do the job just as well, if not better.

I'll be honest: I'm not as good at delegating as I should be. It took me many years before I was willing to hand off anything to do with the firm. But as I grew busier, it was either work seven days a week and do the admin myself, or trust that I could make a good hire. The shift in my mindset has freed me up to focus on the big picture: client-facing work, strategy, and everything that keeps the practice moving forward and growing.

So, if you take away one thing from this section, when you're ready, hire someone who can do the work you need them to do, and if they're good, keep them. Until then, get help from people you trust. Delegating the admin is one of the most important things you can do to avoid burnout, grow, and actually enjoy your practice.

Growing your practice isn't just about great legal work—it's also about being accessible, reliable, and building strong relationships with clients and referral partners. When people can reach you, trust you, and feel respected, they'll continue sending others your way. Take care of the relationships you've already earned, and your referrals will multiply.

When your practice starts to grow, and referrals increase, the next challenge isn't getting new clients—it's managing the workload in a way that keeps you effective, present, and balanced. And that's where the business side of running a law practice becomes just as important as the legal work itself.

The bottom line is, success isn't just measured in cases won or revenue generated—it's measured in memories, connection, and time well spent. Build the practice, yes, but don't forget to also build the life you envisioned when you took the leap.

CHAPTER 11

THE ENDGAME: FROM LEGACY TO LEVERAGE

In my world, I've unfortunately seen too many criminal lawyers whose practices vanish when they retire or pass away. It's sad to witness everything they've worked for disappear in an instant, literally gone in the blink of an eye.

Take a good friend of mine, for example—a very prominent, well-respected criminal defense attorney. He was beloved in the legal community and had a thriving career spanning over fifty years. But then, he passed away in his eighties.

Here's what often happens next: His phone number, once a direct line to his highly sought-after counsel, becomes just another number in the directory. His email account, previously buzzing with urgent requests and case updates, will eventually be ignored and might end up being reassigned to someone else. It's a stark and somewhat bleak reality.

I've seen many attorneys who either didn't plan for the future of their business or simply wound down their operations without a clear strategy. Some kept working right up to the end and then moved their referral sources and rainmaking skills somewhere else without considering how to preserve their legacy and profitability. Don't fall into those traps. Once you're ready to transition out of your practice, you need to be proactive about your exit strategy.

Being motivated about your endgame is essential. It's about ensuring the value you've created over the years doesn't just fade away when you hang 'em up. Whether it's structuring a succession plan or finding a way to merge or sell your practice, taking steps to secure the future of your business is vital. It ensures your hard work and all those relationships continue to benefit others, even when you're no longer at the helm.

If you've followed along with this book, you've learned how to become successful enough so you're not walking away empty-handed at sixty-five. I've shown you how to approach the door, and now it's time to walk through it—exiting your practice with something substantial in hand, which wouldn't be possible if you weren't a rainmaker.

Let's talk about leveraging your superpowers, the unique talents that make you stand out. For some attorneys, their superpower is rainmaking, the ability to attract and retain clients, which is a highly sought-after skill. Consider using this superpower to get another firm to acquire you. The more you network and know people in different practices, and they understand your skill as a rainmaker, the greater the chance of an acquisition. That's one solid exit strategy right there!

But what if rainmaking isn't your only strength? Perhaps you're also an exceptional lawyer. Maybe you're not the top rainmaker, but you're reliable in that arena, and you excel in legal practice. This combination adds significant value to your profile.

Now, imagine you're ready to retire or significantly cut back; you've been a decent rainmaker and a great lawyer, but you're tired of the administrative hassles and just want to handle the cases you're really interested in working on. Perhaps you crave a simpler life where you can focus on what you do best: practicing law without the extra headaches. That's a compelling reason to consider transitioning your practice to a firm that can benefit from your expertise and relieve you of the admin burdens you no longer wish to manage.

This chapter will help you understand how to utilize your strengths to create a graceful and profitable exit from your law practice. Whether it's your exceptional rainmaking abilities, your legal expertise, or both, knowing how to market these skills can set you up for a rewarding next chapter (pun intended).

THE TRANSITION AND SELLING THE PRACTICE

When it comes to transitioning out of your law practice, you essentially have two options. Option one is to just let it die with you. Option two is to allow what you've built to continue to grow and flourish, perhaps as part of someone else's portfolio. This can be a way to help another group of people succeed, and, in a way, it's about leaving a legacy for your family.

Personally, I'd love to join a firm and have the satisfaction of teaching its people to become rainmakers. That would be really cool, right? Plus, I could have a lot of fun trying cases I'm really interested in. They could be civil cases they bring in, and criminal cases I bring in.

I'm still trying to figure out the best way to transition, but I've got some pretty good ideas. For many lawyers, especially those in civil law, you've probably heard of the term "book of business." These lawyers have companies and institutions that regularly hire them—a book of clients who will continue to hire the firm for different matters over time. So, when they retire, their book of business, those clients, have tangible value to someone who might want to buy them out and take over their practice.

Unfortunately, it's a bit different for criminal defense firms like mine, even family law firms like yours. The clients aren't institutions like IBM; they're individuals who've found themselves on the wrong side of the law. While some clients might return or refer others, there's no traditional book of business that can be easily transferred. This makes the endgame much harder for certain types of lawyers compared to civil attorneys with a large, bankable book of business.

In my case, if a younger criminal defense lawyer who wanted to learn how to become a rainmaker were to join my practice, I'd stay on long enough to help mentor them on both the legal practice and client acquisition. The attorney could come from the outside, with this plan in place when they join the firm. But it could also be the associate attorney hired several years ago, who was aware that this opportunity might exist. When I finally leave, the lawyer taking over my practice will be as skilled as I am at acquiring clients and referral sources.

I'd introduce the new lawyer to all my contacts, teach them the strategies I've used to establish and maintain my referral sources, and walk them through the nuances of my practice. It's a bit different than other types of law, but it's how I'd likely handle it. Transition strategies for different types of attorneys need to be more personalized and hands-on, reflecting the unique nature of the practice and its clientele.

YOUR SUPERPOWER

At the end of our careers, each of us probably has a particular talent that could be incredibly useful to an up-and-coming firm. For me, I like to think it's my trial and rainmaking skills. I've done a lot of serious and complicated criminal jury trials with good results against experienced prosecutors who really know their stuff. And I like to think I know how to effectively network in a way to keep the practice growing.

While there are some very good civil trial lawyers, most aren't as experienced as I am in trial work because it's not typically what they do. And, very few combine that skill with rainmaking. When you can see the finish line of your career, you're not just talented, you're super talented.

And you'll hopefully have one or two areas where you're among the best in your town. That's your leverage. For example, if you have substantial trial experience and are a great rainmaker, could you help a big firm? Of course, and so long as they know about you, it makes sense they'd want to bring you aboard.

If you're not sitting on a big book of business to sell, then you've got to make sure potential partners know you're a big-time rainmaker and a skilled lawyer. It's crucial that people in your circle, and the circle next to yours, recognize you're really good at what you do *and* are successful.

As you start to approach the age when you're thinking about exiting, showcase your success to potential buyers. Teach, write a book, share your rainmaking skills with others; become an expert for media outlets, or become the person other lawyers go to for advice. It's all about making it known in the community that you are among the best at what you do in court and rainmaking, because once that's established, everything else starts to fall into place.

JOINING A BIGGER FIRM

If you head over to my LinkedIn profile, you'll see it is optimized for my exit strategy. If a firm sees it, they'll think, "Wow, we could bring this guy in. His salary will pay for itself. We get a good lawyer who will not only help us win trials and make us money, but he'll also teach our other lawyers how to be rainmakers. They'll start bringing in more business, too." It's a win-win.

The idea is that the outflow of salary to you will be more than made up by the amount of business you bring in, and by the other successes the firm will experience. These include winning trials and developing associates who become more skilled and valuable. This strategy turns you into an asset beyond just the cases you work on; it makes you a cornerstone for the firm's reputation, growth, and success.

And here's why joining a big law firm is a solid exit strategy: It significantly reduces admin duties. Even with the great help I have, I'd like even fewer admin duties. So, the idea of joining a new firm where I can shed those admin duties is tempting. No more choosing workers' compensation insurance, picking legal software, or hiring and firing staff. To me, the value of losing these tasks is immense.

Let's say I want to work forty to fifty hours a week, and at sixty-five, being relieved of admin duties could reduce my hours to thirty to thirty-five. What would I do with all that extra time? I'd focus on networking and relationship-building, which I excel at. Imagine the impact a good rainmaker could make on a top-notch law firm with an additional ten to fifteen hours dedicated solely to acquiring new referral sources and client acquisition.

This is a major selling point to any interested firm. Help them be better at whatever you excel at. But no matter what it is, your extra time away from admin will be spent on marketing and networking, which will provide substantial value to the acquiring firm. Be sure to communicate this to a law firm interested in you.

At most law firms, only the equity partners really understand networking. When you are acquired and become part of a new firm, if the new clients you bring in will cover your salary, and you're able to teach a few of their attorneys your superior networking skills, they'll understand and pay to bring you aboard, given how much it benefits the entire firm.

So, as part of my exit strategy, I'm not just bringing my skills as a trial lawyer to a new firm; I'm also bringing my ability to make their lawyers better rainmakers. Plus, as a partner, I'll be rainmaking for the firm, not just for myself. And the firm gets the majority of everything I bring in.

You do need to go in as an equity partner. Clients, especially good ones, expect to see your name on the door if you're good. It's not about ego; it's about recognition. Potential clients and referral sources are more impressed when they meet a named partner, who can also command higher hourly rates. So, if I join a law firm and give them the benefit of my treasure, my name needs to be on the door. This isn't just beneficial for me; it's required to attract clients.

A NEW WHITE-COLLAR PRACTICE

If you're like me, a rainmaker without a typical book of business, then this book will explore what you can do to ensure all your hard work doesn't vanish the day you retire. You definitely don't want to be the lawyer pacing the courthouse in his seventies. So, as you plan your exit strategy after successfully running your own firm, what's your plan for those final five years? For me, it's to wind down, so when I'm seventy, I'm only handling several cases a year that I'm passionate about. Sound like a plan? So, how do we make that happen?

The strategy I favor is to be acquired by a large or mid-sized firm. In addition to helping them try their civil cases, as a white-collar criminal defense attorney, I could start their white-collar practice. And no matter what type of law you practice, like me, you can teach their lawyers how to be rainmakers, and bring in and groom your own successor.

Let's say you're a family law attorney, you bring in a lot of business, and you've tried a lot of cases over the years. When it comes to planning your exit strategy, we'll have many of the same "book of business" issues. Our goal should be to monetize the sale of our practices to bigger firms because we can help them.

Say you join a larger firm that does not have a family law practice. Well, you can bet prior to your joining them they referred out those cases. Think about the fees they lost—their partners have certainly thought about it, that's why they brought you in.

Next, consider the risk they face that those clients they referred out for a divorce or child custody dispute would be stolen by that other firm.

Here's the game plan I would outline to a firm interested in adding you for family law:

- Right away, you, with the firm's help, will look for your eventual successor. This attorney must have the tools necessary to be an effective trial lawyer and the personality and drive to become a great rainmaker. This attorney will be under your wing for however long you remain with the firm.
- With your trial experience, you'll help the law firm try the cases they are already bringing in. Most likely, as a family law attorney, or in my case, a criminal defense attorney, you'll have more experience than any of their attorneys. You bring value.
- With your knowledge of family law, the family law bench, other family law attorneys, and perhaps even family law mediators, you'll be able to help the firm launch a new family law department. Now, the firm no longer needs to refer those cases out, and they become more valuable to their own client base and network. You add even more value.
- You will work with their attorneys, especially your designated successor, on developing rainmaking skills. It

> can be for the types of cases the firm currently handles, family law cases, criminal defense, or whatever it may be. You add significant value, especially in today's world, where market share is declining for larger firms.

Outline a specific plan for beginning the firm's family law department. If I were adding a white-collar criminal defense practice, I know exactly the type of attorney I can help recruit and develop into an effective trial attorney. And I understand the right personality, character, and drive needed in that lawyer so they can become a top-notch rainmaker and, someday, an equity partner at the firm. Your successor should be up and running within a few years, and you'll still be there to lend a hand.

Here is how I imagine it for myself: XYZ firm is a thriving national law firm, with a variety of litigation and transactional practices. But the economy is flat, their client base is stagnant, and a couple of partners have left and taken some big clients with them.

To remain competitive, XYZ needs to be innovative—to think outside the box. They keep hearing about high-profile white-collar criminal cases that command good fees, and decide their firm is known enough that they would have a chance to bring them in if they had the right attorney there, so they decide to start a white-collar department. Ideally, they'd like to bring in an effective trial lawyer and rainmaker to build the department and even to help them on some of their own trials. Bingo—endgame accomplished.

Just for fun, let's pretend that at the very last interview before the hiring decision, the firm's managing partner asks me to describe my first two months at the firm. Here's my answer.

- Weeks one and two – I sit down with the hiring partners and discuss a list of five attorneys I already have in mind who would be great fits for criminal trial work and have the right personalities it takes to succeed as a rainmaker. I'd suggest taking our time and finding the right person for the position. I'd begin gauging interest.
- Weeks three and four – We'd go over a list of upcoming civil trials where the firm would like my help; I'd be introduced to the attorney in charge of the case, and begin looking at whether we're on track to be ready for trial, and if not, what needs to be done.
- Weeks five and six – With the more immediate needs being handled, we can now discuss the new white-collar department. What types of cases will we handle? E.g., will we take DUIs and other criminal cases? We will talk about the culture of the department and be sure the associate we hired understands how we onboard cases, thank referral sources, communicate with clients and the courts, network, and how we will make this new department visible to the legal community.

  At the same time, I will have already begun introducing my successor to my referral sources and people in the court system. With the firm's assistance, we'll create a marketing plan directed to the firm's clients and current referral sources, describing the firm's new practice, and create a plan where the firm's attorneys can generate buzz within their own networks for the white-collar practice.

- Weeks seven and eight – We'll identify the attorneys at the firm whom the equity partners feel have the potential to be successful rainmakers. We will set up internal networking meetings, have the attorneys jump into different marketing groups where they would promote the firm's primary area of practice, but also let it be known that the firm has a high-end white-collar practice. My successor and I would already be in at least two networking groups each, promoting the firm's new white-collar practice.

Once we have everything going smoothly, we'd host a firm-wide networking event, whether it be disguised as a holiday party, summer get-together, or whatever it may be, where everyone in the legal community is invited. We'd get the word to the bench and to the entire legal community that our firm is growing and has a new practice where potential referral sources can feel comfortable sending business.

Fast forward five years, and things are booming—the white-collar practice is thriving. Now, as I start to step back, I'll still handle several cases a year—just the ones I really want. And all the while, I'm still a rainmaker, maintaining and sharing all of my connections with the firm. Meanwhile, my successor, who has learned the right way to network and grow as an attorney, will be adding substantial value to the firm. There will eventually come a time when I'm done with the legal work, and by then, my successor will have it all under control.

Does any of this seem far-fetched or unreasonable? No, it's not. The firm must buy in, but that's on me when I agree to join them. The successor must work out, and although there is no guarantee, if I bring in someone willing to learn, this endgame will be a huge success.

The firm you join can be a large national firm or perhaps a smaller firm looking to grow and diversify. This is an endgame strategy you can start preparing for whenever you're ready. If nothing else, just start the conversation with friends who own law firms. It's an easy chat about the potential benefits of adding a white-collar practice, including bringing in clients, sharing profits, and elevating the firm's status.

You now have the knowledge and the tools required to go out on your own, be successful, and then successfully and profitably transition out of your otherwise difficult-to-sell practice.

FINAL THOUGHT

I was wearing an olive-green three-piece suit the day I got fired.

My friends joked that because of my height, I looked like a giant green banana in that suit. They weren't wrong. And although my dad wasn't a lawyer, he was an engineer who always said, "Lawyers wear dark suits. That's what people expect. Not green. Not yellow. You want to be wearing dark blue, pinstripe, with a red tie."

Believe it or not, in the early '90s, those crazy colored suits were actually in style. But that morning, I wasn't thinking about fashion; I was just going to work like any other day, walking into a law office where I'd climbed my way up to senior attorney, making the highest salary, and getting the best trials. The partners and I were friends. We always had a blast talking about sports and whatever interesting cases we had.

Prior to the day I was fired, the firm I was with was appointed hundreds of cases a year, everything from misdemeanors to felonies, murders, gang cases, and three-strikes. It was steady, serious work—I literally did dozens of trials a year.

Out of nowhere, because of a budget crisis, the county created a second public defender's office. Just like that, we lost 90 percent of our business and would not survive.

I was in my office working when one of the assistants came in and said, "The partners would like to see you." I walked in, and both partners were sitting there. Normally, we'd be joking around, talking about the Lakers. But that day, they were solemn.

They said, "We hate to do this, Bob. This has nothing to do with your work. We just don't have the contract anymore. We have to let you go."

I remember being stunned. Not angry, just in disbelief. I didn't take it personally. But my first thought was, *How am I going to cover everything next month*? Followed by, *What about medical insurance? That's going to get expensive.*

I felt empty. The surprise, the disappointment, the shock of it. I'm pretty sure I sat there for a minute, and no one in the room said a word. A couple of thoughts flashed across my mind: *Is this really happening? What am I going to do?* I knew if I wanted to stay in criminal defense and continue to get lots of trials, which is what I love, I had one option: I had to start my own firm. I decided right there that's what I would do. I thanked them for the great experience I gained while working there, and wished them both luck. My last paycheck would be in two weeks.

I remember walking to my car that day thinking, *Alright. It's The Hartmann Law Firm now. There's no other choice.* It was tempting to feel sorry for myself, but that's not me. I'm a lawyer, I can make something work.

That night, I thought about all the judges I knew well, some of whom helped create the lists of private attorneys who were appointed on various criminal cases when the two public defender offices had conflicts. I knew I needed to talk to them immediately.

The next day, I literally went from courtroom to courtroom, asking if I could speak with the judge in chambers. I told them what happened, I'd been let go, and was now available for court appointments. "If the Public Defenders can't take a case, I'd appreciate it if you'd keep me in mind." It was embarrassing to say out loud, but I got it done.

Then I reached out to the guy who managed the lists and asked to be added to all of them.

Also in the first week, I called a friend who had a personal injury practice and told him what happened. To my surprise, he said, "Work out of our office. You can have a space rent-free for a month." It was perfect. They didn't practice criminal law so they could send me referrals.

From there, I started telling every lawyer I knew I was on my own. And, I reached out to everyone in my rather limited network. Before I was fired, I handled court-appointed cases, so I never had a need to develop a network. But then, I let them know I was available for cases, offered referral fees, and started picking up court appearance work for $50 to $100 an hour, whatever it took to pay the bills.

I did that for a year or two. I wasn't yet in any networking groups. I didn't even know about those. I went to bar association events, a waste. What helped was building trust, one lawyer at a time. As I met more people, the work started to trickle in.

I think a year later, I received a referral to handle a murder case. I believe I charged $75,000, and my heart was racing while I waited for the check to come in. That case alone was enough to cover my mortgage for months. I thought, *Okay. I'm going to be okay. I can breathe.*

It all evolved organically: from one day being fired, then to telling judges and friends, to slowly expanding out and letting the whole community know. What amazed me was how many people genuinely wanted to help. People don't want you to starve when you go out on your own. It was true for me, and I'll never forget it.

And that's how I survived getting fired. I had no financial help. I had a mortgage and a car payment. I did whatever it took. I showed up. I shook hands. I said hello to every judge, every D.A., every defense lawyer, every P.I. lawyer, every employment lawyer. I started sending letters, even holiday cards. And eventually, I figured it out: You have to stay in touch. You can't disappear.

The first semi-big purchase I made, once I felt like I'd landed on my feet? New suits.

CLOSING ARGUMENT

Thank you for reading through to the final page. If this book has offered insight or support in your work, please consider leaving a review on the retailer's site. Your feedback makes a difference—and it helps other lawyers find the book too.

You now know what took me decades to figure out: Success doesn't happen because you're the smartest lawyer in the room or because you line your office walls with degrees and awards. It happens because you show up, again and again—in courtrooms, in networking meetings, in conversations that feel awkward at first. *And don't forget empathy* because it is the lifeblood of your business.

The bottom line is that success happens because you build relationships, treat people well, follow up, and earn trust one handshake and one case at a time.

Someday, you'll close your last file. The phone will ring less often. And you'll realize your reputation, your relationships, and your rainmaking ability were always the true equity in your business.

Case Closed.

ACKNOWLEDGMENTS

My gratitude goes to Melanie Herschorn for your support, patience, insight, and help; you've always kept me moving forward when the finish line seemed far away.

My thanks as well to Gary Johnson for your friendship and thoughtful suggestions, which helped make these pages far superior to the first draft. I'm also grateful to Michael Ashley, Ivan Gonzalez, Randall Holbrook, and Marc Weisberg for your support and hard work in bringing to life many of the marketing concepts discussed in the book.

I'm especially thankful to Marcela Robledo for your support and patience over the years while I grew The Hartmann Law Firm, for my parents, Manfred and Lynn Hartmann, who made possible my career, and to my brother Larry Hartmann, who is always there with a fishing or whale watching trip when I need a break.

Others who I appreciate more than each of you will ever know are Stephanie Barrera, Terrie Beals, Paloma Cornejo, Tony and Carol Erenyi, Ginny Fisher, Stanley Friedman Esq., Christina Garkovich, Ron and Vicki Geisler, Greg and Susan Kassel, Jenni and Adam Nering, Cynthia Sender, Sandeep Shah Esq., and Julie Tran.

Law school taught us how to read and write a contract. But we learned nothing about entrepreneurship. With Covid, AI, and the way in which the legal world is evolving, it is more important than ever for attorneys to understand they're never going to achieve the work-life-wealth balance they dream of while working for others in a law firm.

ABOUT THE AUTHOR

Robert Hartmann isn't just a lawyer. He is a seasoned advocate who understands that great results for his clients come not only from legal skill, but from judgment, credibility, determination, and the ability to navigate both the law and the business of law when it matters most.

Only a small percentage of attorneys ever earn the title of Certified Criminal Law Specialist by the California State Bar. Out of more than 120,000 licensed lawyers, fewer than 400 hold this prestigious designation, and Bob is one of them.

With over 200 jury trials in state and federal court and a legal career spanning nearly four decades, he is a nationally recognized white-collar criminal defense attorney, representing individuals in all types of criminal cases including complex state and federal matters involving the Department of Justice, Securities and Exchange Commission, Internal Revenue Service, Commodity Futures Trading Commission, and other government agencies, as well as local and state prosecuting agencies.

Bob began practicing law in 1987 and founded The Hartmann Law Firm in 1991, building a reputation for strategic excellence, meticulous preparation, and fearless advocacy. He is known for providing direct, honest counsel, maintaining 24/7 accessibility for clients facing high-stakes legal challenges, and ensuring that his clients are not just represented—but truly heard—within the legal system. When the consequences are serious, clients trust Bob to protect their reputation, freedom, and future.

In addition to his private practice, he has served as a Superior Court Judge Pro Tem, adjunct law professor, and legal commentator, bringing a broad and balanced perspective to the practice of criminal defense.

Over the course of his career, Bob has been consistently recognized by judges, prosecutors, and other defense attorneys for his expertise and is frequently sought out by lawyers for his depth of experience in complex criminal litigation. Beyond the courtroom, he is committed to community service, including leadership roles with organizations supporting at-risk youth.

A champion poker player, who once competed and cashed in the World Series of Poker, Bob resides in Southern California.

www.ingramcontent.com/pod-product-compliance
Lightning Source LLC
LaVergne TN
LVHW090358210926
848480LV00002B/388